FOREWORD

We wish to thank the club secretaries of the Scottish Premier League, the Scottish League and the Highland League for their assistance in providing the information contained in this guide. We also wish to thank Bob Budd for the cover artwork and Tony Brown for providing the Cup Statistics (www.soccerdata.com).

When using this guide, readers should note that most clubs also extend the child concessionary prices to include Senior Citizens.

Additional copies of this guide can be obtained directly from us at the address shown on the facing page. Alternatively, orders may be placed securely via our web site – www.soccer-books.co.uk

Finally, we would like to wish our readers a happy and safe spectating season.

John Robinson
EDITOR

ROT

CONTENTS

COME AND VISIT THE HOME OF SCOTTISH FOOTBALL –

SCOTTISH FOOTBALL MUSEUM

at Hampden

See over 2,500 exhibits in 14 Galleries and walk amongst Scotland's most famous footballing legends in the Scottish Football Hall of Fame. It's a day out that you will always remember, spent at the spiritual home of Scottish football – Hampden Park. The exhibits are relics of Scottish History and the story is told with the help of men and women who made football what it is today. Spend a day enjoying Scotland's football heritage, remembering the legends that inspire champions and you can also add a tour of Hampden Stadium itself to your visit.

Here are just a few of the great things to see…

1872 Scotland v England Match Ticket
  from the world's first football international

The Scottish Cup
  the world's oldest surviving national football trophy

The "Wembley Wizards" Ball
  from Scotland's famous 5-1 victory over England in 1928

The British International Trophy
  trophy from the World's oldest international football tournament

Old Dressing Room
  part of the famous "home dressing room" from the 1903 building

Hampden Press Box
  a section of the old South Stand press box

Dalglish Silver Cap
  commemorating "King Kenny's" 100th International appearance for Scotland

Jimmy McGrory's Boots
  Scotland's most prolific goalscorer

To book:

Phone (0141) 616-6139

or check out:

www.scottishfootballmuseum.org.uk

MUSEUM OPENING TIMES

Monday to Saturday 10.00am – 5.00pm

Sunday 11.00am – 5.00pm

MUSEUM ADMISSION

Adults £5.50

Concessions £2.75

(Children ages 5-16, Senior Citizens, Students & unemployed)

Children under 5 .... FREE

STADIUM TOUR

Adults £6.00

(£3.00 when visiting the Museum)

Concessions £3.00

(£1.50 when visiting the museum)

EDITOR
John Robinson

Sixteenth Edition

British Library Cataloguing in Publication Data
A catalogue record for this book is available from the British Library

ISBN: 978-1-86223-160-3

Copyright © 2007, SOCCER BOOKS LIMITED (01472 696226)
72 St. Peter's Avenue, Cleethorpes, N.E. Lincolnshire, DN35 8HU, England
Web site   http://www.soccer-books.co.uk
e-mail   info@soccer-books.co.uk

Manufactured in the UK by LPPS Ltd, Wellingborough, NN8 3PJ

HAMPDEN –
SCOTLAND'S NATIONAL STADIUM

Opened: 1903
Location: Hampden Park, Mount Florida, Glasgow
G42 9BA
Telephone Nº: (0141) 620-4000
Fax Number: (0141) 620-4001

Record Attendance: 150,239
(Scotland vs England, 17th April 1937)
Pitch Size: 115 × 75 yards
Ground Capacity: 52,063 (All seats)
Web Site: www.hampdenpark.co.uk

GENERAL INFORMATION
Car Parking: 536 spaces + 39 disabled spaces at Stadium
Coach Parking: Stadium Coach Park
Nearest Railway Station: Mount Florida and King's Park
(both are 5 minutes walk)
Nearest Bus Station: Buchanan Street
Nearest Police Station: Aikenhead Road, Glasgow
Police Telephone Nº: (0141) 532-4900

DISABLED INFORMATION
Wheelchairs: Accommodated in disabled spectators
sections at all levels in the South Stand, particularly levels 1
and 4 where special catering and toilet facilities are available.
Disabled Toilets: Available
Commentaries are available for the blind
Contact: (0141) 620-4000

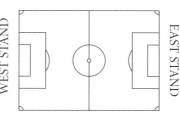

Travelling Supporters' Information:
Routes: From the South: Take the A724 to the Cambuslang Road and at Eastfield branch left into Main Street and follow
through Burnhill Street and Westmuir Place into Prospecthill Road. Turn left into Aikenhead Road and right into Mount Annan
for Kinghorn Drive and the Stadium; From the South: Take the A77 Fenwick Road, through Kilmarnock Road into Pollokshaws
Road then turn right into Langside Avenue. Pass through Battle Place to Battlefield Road and turn left into Cathcart Road. Turn
right into Letherby Drive, right into Carmunnock Road and 1st left into Mount Annan Drive for the Stadium; From the North &
East: Exit M8 Junction 15 and passing Infirmary on left proceed into High Street and cross the Albert Bridge into Crown Street.
Join Cathcart Road and proceed South until it becomes Carmunnock Road. Turn left into Mount Annan Drive and left again into
Kinghorn Drive for the Stadium.

THE SCOTTISH FOOTBALL ASSOCIATION

Founded

1873

Address

National Stadium, Hampden Park,
Mount Florida, Glasgow   G42 9BA

Web Site

www.scottishfa.co.uk

Phone

(0141) 616-6000

Fax

(0141) 616-6001

THE SCOTTISH PREMIER LEAGUE

Address

National Stadium, Hampden Park,
Mount Florida, Glasgow   G42 9BA

Web Site   www.scotprem.com

Phone   (0141) 620-4140
Fax   (0141) 620-4141

Clubs for the 2007/2008 Season

ABERDEEN FC

Founded: 1903 (**Entered League**: 1904)
Nickname: 'The Dons'
Ground: Pittodrie Stadium, Pittodrie Street, Aberdeen AB24 5QH
Ground Capacity: 21,431 (all seats)
Record Attendance: 45,061 (13/3/54)
Pitch Size: 115 × 72 yards

Colours: Red shirts and shorts
Telephone Nº: (01224) 650400
Ticket Office: 0871 983-1903
Fax Number: (01224) 644173
Web Site: www.afc.co.uk

GENERAL INFORMATION

Car Parking: Beach Promenade, King Street and Golf Road
Coach Parking: At the rear of the Stadium
Nearest Railway Station: Aberdeen (1 mile)
Nearest Bus Station: Aberdeen
Club Shop: At the ground and also Bridge Street, Aberdeen
Opening Times: 9.00am to 5.00pm
Telephone Nº: (01224) 642800 or 212797
Police Telephone Nº: (0845) 600-5700

GROUND INFORMATION

Away Supporters' Entrances & Sections:
Park Road entrance for the South Stand East

ADMISSION INFO (2007/2008 PRICES)

Adult Seating: £16.00 to £26.00
Child Seating: £5.00 to £10.00 (Under 12's)
Senior Citizen/Under 18s/Students: £8.00 to £18.00
Prices vary according to the category of the game
Programme Price: £2.50

DISABLED INFORMATION

Wheelchairs: 7 spaces available in the South Stand for away fans. 26 spaces in total for home fans although 21 of these are currently held by season ticket holders leaving just 5 spaces available on general sale
Helpers: One helper admitted per wheelchair
Prices: Free of charge for wheelchair disabled and helpers
Disabled Toilets: Available in the Richard Donald Stand, the Merkland Stand, in the Away Section and in a new toilet block at the Richard Donald Stand entrance
Contact: 0871 983-1903 (Bookings are necessary)

Travelling Supporters' Information:
Routes: From the City Centre, travel along Union Street then turn left into King Street. The Stadium is about ½ mile along King Street (A92) on the right-hand side.

CELTIC FC

Founded: 1888 (**Entered League**: 1890)
Nickname: 'The Bhoys' 'The Hoops'
Ground: Celtic Park, Glasgow   G40 3RE
Ground Capacity: 60,355 (All seats)
Record Attendance: 92,000 (1/1/38)
Pitch Size: 115 × 74 yards

Colours: Green & White hooped shirts, White shorts
General Telephone Nº: 0871 226-1888
General Fax Number: (0141) 551-8106
Ticket Office Fax Nº: (0141) 551-4223
Web Site: www.celticfc.net

GENERAL INFORMATION

Car Parking: Limited on Matchdays to those with a Valid Car Park Pass. Otherwise, street parking
Coach Parking: Gallowgate, Fielden Street, Biggar Street and Nuneaton Street
Nearest Railway Station: Bellgrove (10 minutes walk)
Nearest Bus Stop: Outside of the ground
Club Shop: Superstore at Celtic Park. Also in Glasgow: 21 High Street; 215 Sauchiehall Street; 154 Argyle Street; Terminal 1, Glasgow Airport. Elsewhere: 5 West Blackhall Street, Greenock; 24 West Mall, The Plaza, East Kilbride Shopping Centre; 34 Frederick Street, Edinburgh; 74 Sylvania Way, The Clyde Shopping Centre, Clydebank; 72 Main Street, Coatbridge; Unit 26, The Thistle Centre, Stirling; 30/34 Ann Street, Belfast; 4/6 Bishop St., Derry; Unit 10, 125 Upper Abbey St., Dublin. Also in selected Debenhams outlets throughout Scotland and Ireland
Opening Times: Please contact the Superstore for details
Telephone Nº: (0141) 551-4231 (Superstore)
Police Telephone Nº: (0141) 532-4600

GROUND INFORMATION

Away Supporters' Entrances & Sections:
Kinloch Street Turnstiles for the East Stand

ADMISSION INFO (2007/2008 PRICES)

Adult Seating: £24.00 – £35.00
Child/Senior Citizen Seating: £14.00 – £17.00
Programme Price: £2.00

DISABLED INFORMATION

Wheelchairs: 141 spaces for home fans and 6 spaces for away fans in the North Stand and East Stand
Helpers: 144 helpers admitted in total
Prices: £3.00 – £5.00 subject to availability (there is a waiting list). This covers a disabled fan and a helper
Disabled Toilets: 5 available in the North Stand, 2 in the East Stand and 3 in the South West Stand
Contact: 0871 226-1888   (Bookings are necessary)

Travelling Supporters' Information:
Routes: From the South and East: Take the A74 London Road towards the City Centre, Celtic Park is on the right about ½ mile past the Belvidere Hospital and the ground is clearly visible; From the West: Take the A74 London Road from the City Centre and turn left about ½ mile past Bridgeton Station.

DUNDEE UNITED FC

Founded: 1909 (**Entered League**: 1910)
Former Names: Dundee Hibernians FC
Nickname: 'The Terrors'
Ground: Tannadice Park, Tannadice Street, Dundee, DD3 7JW
Ground Capacity: 14,223 (all seats)
Record Attendance: 28,000 (November 1966)

Pitch Size: 110 × 72 yards
Colours: Tangerine shirts with Black shorts
Telephone Nº: (01382) 833166
Ticket Office: (01382) 833166
Fax Number: (01382) 889398
Web Site: www.dundeeunitedfc.co.uk

GENERAL INFORMATION
Car Parking: Street Parking and Melrose Car Park
Coach Parking: Gussie Park (home coaches)
Nearest Railway Station: Dundee (20 minutes walk)
Nearest Bus Station: Dundee
Club Shop: In Tannadice Street
Opening Times: Monday to Saturday 9.00am–5.00pm
Telephone Nº: (01382) 833166
Police Telephone Nº: (01382) 223200

GROUND INFORMATION
Away Supporters' Entrances & Sections:
Turnstiles 7-16 for South Stand & Fair Play Stand

ADMISSION INFO (2007/2008 PRICES)
Adult Seating: £19.00 – £25.00
Child Seating: £10.00 – £13.00
Note: Prices vary depending on the category of the game
Programme Price: £2.50 (Price may change this season)

DISABLED INFORMATION
Wheelchairs: Accommodated in the George Fox Stand and the East and West Stands
Helpers: Please phone the club for details
Prices: Please phone the club for details
Disabled Toilets: Available in the George Fox Stand and in the East and West Stands
Contact: (01382) 833166 (Bookings are necessary)

Travelling Supporters' Information:
Routes: From the South or West: Travel via Perth and take the A90 to Dundee. Once in Dundee join the Kingsway (ring road) and follow until the third exit marked "Football Traffic", then turn right onto Old Glamis Road. Follow the road to join Provost Road then turn left into Sandeman Street for the ground; From the North: Follow the A90 from Aberdeen and join the Kingsway (ring road). At the first set of traffic lights turn right into Clepington Road and follow into Arklay Street before turning right into Tannadice Street for the ground.

FALKIRK FC

Founded: 1876   (**Entered League**: 1902)
Nickname: 'The Bairns'
Ground: Falkirk Stadium, Westfield, Falkirk,
FK2 9DX
Ground Capacity: 7,190 (All seats)
Pitch Size: 112 x 75 yards

Colours: Navy Blue shirts with White shorts
Telephone Nº: (01324) 624121
Ticket Office: (01324) 624121
Fax Number: (01324) 612418
Web Site: www.falkirkfc.co.uk

GENERAL INFORMATION
Car Parking: A large Car Park is adjacent
Coach Parking: Available nearby
Nearest Railway Station: Falkirk Grahamston (1 mile)
Nearest Bus Station: Falkirk (1 mile)
Club Shop: Kirk Wynd, Falkirk
Opening Times: 9.00am to 5.00pm
Telephone Nº: (01324) 639366
Police Telephone Nº: (01324) 562112

GROUND INFORMATION
Away Supporters' Entrances & Sections:
North Stand

ADMISSION INFO (2007/2008 PRICES)
Adult Seating: £19.00 – £24.00
Child Seating: £13.00
Concessionary Seating: £13.00
Programme Price: £2.50 (Price may change this season)

DISABLED INFORMATION
Wheelchairs: Accommodated
Helpers: Admitted
Prices: Free for the disabled. Normal prices for helpers
Disabled Toilets: Available
Contact: (01324) 624121   (Bookings are necessary)

Travelling Supporters' Information:
Routes: Exit the M9 at Junction 6 and take the A904 towards Falkirk. Continue into Falkirk at the Westfield/Laurieston roundabout along Grangemouth Road and take the first right into Alexander Avenue. Then take the 2nd right into Westfield Street and the ground is on the right.

GRETNA FC

Gretna FC are playing at Motherwell FC's Fir Park for the 2007/2008 season

Founded: 1946 (**Entered League**: 2002)
Nickname: 'Black and Whites'
Ground: Firpark, Firpark Street, Motherwell, ML1 2QN
Ground Capacity: 13,664 (all seats)
Record Attendance: 35,632 (12/3/52)
Pitch Size: 102 × 68 yards

Colours: Shirts are White with Black trim, White shorts
Telephone Nº: (01461) 337602
Fax Number: (01461) 338047
Web Site: www.gretnafootballclub.co.uk

GENERAL INFORMATION
Car Parking: Street parking and nearby Car Parks
Coach Parking: Orbiston Street
Nearest Railway Station: Airbles (1 mile)
Nearest Bus Station: Motherwell
Club Shop: At Raydale Park, Gretna
Opening Times: Monday to Friday 9.00am to 5.00pm
Telephone Nº: (01698) 338025
Police Telephone Nº: (01698) 483000

GROUND INFORMATION
Away Supporters' Entrances & Sections:
Dalziel Drive entrances for the South Stand

ADMISSION INFO (2007/2008 PRICES)
Adult Seating: £20.00 – £24.00
Child Seating: £10.00 – £12.00
Concessionary Seating: £14.00 – £16.00
Programme Price: £2.50

DISABLED INFORMATION
Wheelchairs: 20 spaces for home fans and 10 spaces for away fans in the South-West enclosure.
Helpers: Admitted
Prices: Please phone the club for information
Disabled Toilets: One available close to the Disabled Area
Contact: (01698) 338009   (Must book 1 week in advance)

Travelling Supporters' Information:
Routes: From the East: Take the A723 into Merry Street and turn left into Brandon Street (1 mile). Follow through to Windmill Hill Street and turn right at the Fire Station into Knowetop Avenue for the ground; From Elsewhere: Exit the M74 at Junction 4 and take the A723 Hamilton Road into the Town Centre. Turn right into West Hamilton Street and follow into Brandon Street – then as from the East.

HEART OF MIDLOTHIAN FC

Founded: 1874 (**Entered League**: 1890)
Nickname: 'The Jam Tarts' 'Jambos'
Ground: Tynecastle Stadium, Gorgie Road,
Edinburgh   EH11 2NL
Ground Capacity: 17,402 (All seats)
Record Attendance: 53,496 (13/1/32)
Pitch Size: 110 × 70 yards

Colours: Maroon shirts with White shorts
Telephone Nº: 0871 663-1874 Option 7
Ticket Office: 0871 663-1874 Option 1
Fax Number: (0131) 200-7222
Web Site: www.heartsfc.co.uk

GENERAL INFORMATION

Car Parking: Street Parking in Robertson Avenue and Westfield Road
Coach Parking: Russell Road
Nearest Railway Station: Edinburgh Haymarket (½ mile)
Nearest Bus Station: St. Andrew's Square
Club Superstore: Gorgie Stand/Tynecastle Terrace
Opening Times: Weekdays 9.30am to 5.30pm, Non-match Saturdays 10.00am–4.00pm, Matchdays 10.00am–1.30pm, Sundays 12.00pm – 4.00pm
Telephone Nº: 0871 663-1874 Option 2
Police Telephone Nº: (0131) 229-2323

GROUND INFORMATION

Away Supporters' Entrances & Sections:
Roseburn Stand entrances and accommodation

ADMISSION INFO (2007/2008 PRICES)

Adult Seating: £13.00 – £38.00
Senior Citizen/Child Seating: £6.00 – £28.00
Note: Prices vary depending on the category of the game but very few seats will be available for most home games
Programme: £3.00

DISABLED INFORMATION

Wheelchairs: 100 spaces available for home and away fans in Wheatfield, Roseburn & Gorgie Stands
Helpers: Admitted
Prices: Normal prices for the disabled. Free for helpers
Disabled Toilets: Available
Contact: 0871 663-1874 Option 7   (Bookings are necessary)

Travelling Supporters' Information:
Routes: From the West: Take the A71 (Ayr Road) into Gorgie Road and the ground is about ¾ mile past Saughton Park on the left; From the North: Take the A90 Queensferry Road and turn right into Drum Brae after about ½ mile. Follow Drum Brae into Meadowplace Road (about 1 mile) then Broomhouse Road to the junction with Calder Road. Turn right, then as from the West; From the South: Take the A702/A703 to the A720 (Oxgangs Road). Turn left and follow the A720 into Wester Hailes Road (2½ miles) until the junction with Calder Road. Turn right, then as from the West.

HIBERNIAN FC

Founded: 1875 (**Entered League**: 1893)
Nickname: 'The Hi-Bees'
Ground: Easter Road Stadium, 12 Albion Place,
Edinburgh EH7 5QG
Ground Capacity: 17,400 (all seats)
Record Attendance: 65,840 (2/1/50)
Pitch Size: 115 × 70 yards

Colours: Green and White shirts with Green shorts
Telephone Nº: (0131) 661-2159
Ticket Office: 0844 844-1875
Fax Number: (0131) 659-6488
Web Site: www.hibernianfc.co.uk

GENERAL INFORMATION

Car Parking: Street parking
Coach Parking: Regent Road (by Police Direction)
Nearest Railway Station: Edinburgh Waverley
(25 minutes walk)
Nearest Bus Station: St. Andrews Square
Club Shop: Famous Five Stand
Opening Times: Monday to Friday 9.00am – 5.00pm,
Saturday Matchdays 9.00am – 3.00pm and ½ hour after the
game. Non-matchday Saturdays 9.00am – 5.00pm, Sundays
11.00am – 4.00pm
Telephone Nº: (0131) 656-7078
Police Telephone Nº: (0131) 554-9350

GROUND INFORMATION

Away Supporters' Entrances & Sections:
South Stand entrances and accommodation

ADMISSION INFO (2007/2008 PRICES)

Adult Seating: £21.00 – £26.00
Child Seating: £11.00
Programme Price: £2.00

DISABLED INFORMATION

Wheelchairs: 56 spaces in the West Stand, 11 spaces in the
Famous Five Stand + 11 spaces in the South Stand
Helpers: One helper admitted per disabled person
Prices: £11.00 each for the disabled and their helpers
Disabled Toilets: 4 available in the Famous Five and South
Stands, 5 available in the West Stand
Contact: (0131) 661-2159 – Ask for Ticket Office Supervisor
(Bookings are necessary for home supporters. Away
Supporters should book and pay through their own club)

Travelling Supporters' Information:
Routes: From the West and North: Take the A90 Queensferry Road to the A902 and continue for 2¼ miles. Turn right into
Great Junction Street and follow into Duke Street then Lochend Road. Turn sharp right into Hawkhill Avenue at Lochend Park
and follow the road into Albion Place for the ground; From the South: Take the A1 through Musselburgh (Milton Road/Willow
Brae/London Road) and turn right into Easter Road after about 2½ miles. Take the 4th right into Albion Road for the ground.

INVERNESS CALEDONIAN THISTLE FC

Founded: 1994 (**Entered League**: 1994)
Former Names: Caledonian Thistle FC
Nickname: 'The Jags' 'Caley'
Ground: Tulloch Caledonian Stadium, East Longman, Inverness IV1 1FF
Ground Capacity: 7,400 (all seats)
Record Attendance: 7,400
Pitch Size: 115 × 75 yards

Colours: Shirts are Royal Blue and Red stripes, Shorts are Royal Blue
Telephone N⁰: (01463) 222880 (Ground)
Ticket Office: (01463) 222880
Fax Number: (01463) 227479
Web Site: www.ictfc.co.uk

GENERAL INFORMATION

Car Parking: At the ground
Coach Parking: At the ground
Nearest Railway Station: Inverness (1 mile)
Nearest Bus Station: Inverness
Club Shop: At the ground
Opening Times: Weekdays and Matchdays 9.00am–5.00pm
Telephone N⁰: (01463) 222880
Police Telephone N⁰: (01463) 715555

GROUND INFORMATION

Away Supporters' Entrances & Sections:
South Stand

ADMISSION INFO (2007/2008 PRICES)

Adult Seating: £15.00 – £27.00
Child Seating: £7.00 – £22.00
Senior Citizen Seating: £13.00 – £22.00
Programme Price: £2.50

DISABLED INFORMATION

Wheelchairs: 52 spaces available in total
Helpers: Admitted
Prices: Free of charge for the disabled and their helpers
Disabled Toilets: Available
Contact: (01463) 222880 (Bookings are necessary)

Travelling Supporters' Information:
Routes: The ground is adjacent to Kessock Bridge. From the South: Take the A9 to Inverness and turn right at the roundabout before the bridge over the Moray Firth; From the North: Take the A9 over the bridge and turn left at the roundabout for the ground.

KILMARNOCK FC

Founded: 1869 (**Entered League**: 1896)
Nickname: 'Killie'
Ground: Rugby Park, Rugby Road, Kilmarnock, Ayrshire KA1 2DP
Record Attendance: 34,246 (17/8/63)
Pitch Size: 115 × 74 yards

Colours: Shirts are Blue with broad White stripes, White shorts
Telephone Nº: (01563) 545300
Fax Number: (01563) 522181
Ground Capacity: 18,128 (all seats)
Web Site: www.kilmarnockfc.co.uk

GENERAL INFORMATION

Car Parking: At the ground (Permit Holders only)
Coach Parking: Fairyhill Road Bus Park
Nearest Railway Station: Kilmarnock (15 minutes walk)
Nearest Bus Station: Kilmarnock (10 minutes walk)
Club Shop: Adjacent to the West Stand at the ground
Opening Times: Monday to Friday 9.00am – 5.00pm, Saturdays 10.00am – 2.00pm (until kick-off on matchdays)
Telephone Nº: (01563) 545310
Police Telephone Nº: (01563) 521188

GROUND INFORMATION

Away Supporters' Entrances & Sections:
Rugby Road turnstiles for the Chadwick Stand

ADMISSION INFO (2007/2008 PRICES)

Adult Seating: £20.00
Concessionary Seating: £14.00
Under-12s Seating: £14.00 (£5.00 in the Moffat Stand)
Note: Prices for games against Rangers & Celtic are £24.00 with only 200 concessionary tickets available at £14.00. These are allocated on a first-come first-served basis
Programme Price: £2.50

DISABLED INFORMATION

Wheelchairs: 15 spaces each for home and away fans in the Main Stand
Helpers: One helper admitted per wheelchair
Prices: £5.00 for the disabled. Helpers £8.00
Disabled Toilets: 2 available in the Chadwick Stand and Moffat Stand
Contact: (01294) 270100 (Bookings are necessary)

Travelling Supporters' Information:
Routes: From Glasgow/Ayr: Take the A77 Kilmarnock Bypass. Exit at the Bellfield Interchange. Take the A71 (Irvine) to the first roundabout then take the A759 (Kilmarnock Town Centre). The ground is ½ mile on the left hand side.

MOTHERWELL FC

Founded: 1886 (**Entered League:** 1893)
Nickname: 'The Well'
Ground: Firpark, Firpark Street, Motherwell, ML1 2QN
Ground Capacity: 13,664 (all seats)
Record Attendance: 35,632 (12/3/52)
Pitch Size: 102 × 68 yards

Colours: Shirts are Amber with a Claret chestband and Claret trim, Shorts are White with Claret trim
Telephone Nº: (01698) 333333
Ticket Office: (01698) 333333
Fax Number: (01698) 338001
Web Site: www.motherwellfc.co.uk

GENERAL INFORMATION

Car Parking: Street parking and nearby Car Parks
Coach Parking: Orbiston Street
Nearest Railway Station: Airbles (1 mile)
Nearest Bus Station: Motherwell
Club Shop: At the ground
Opening Times: Weekdays 9.30am to 4.00pm plus Saturday Matchdays from 9.30am to 5.30pm
Telephone Nº: (01698) 338025
Police Telephone Nº: (01698) 483000

GROUND INFORMATION

Away Supporters' Entrances & Sections:
Dalziel Drive entrances for the South Stand

ADMISSION INFO (2007/2008 PRICES)

Adult Seating: £17.00 – £24.00
Child Seating: £8.00 – £12.00
Concessionary Seating: £12.00 – £16.00
Note: Discounts are available in the Family Section and prices vary depending on the category of the game
Programme Price: £2.00

DISABLED INFORMATION

Wheelchairs: 20 spaces for home fans and 10 spaces for away fans in the South-West enclosure.
Helpers: Admitted
Prices: Please phone the club for information
Disabled Toilets: One available close to the Disabled Area
Contact: (01698) 338009 (Must book 1 week in advance)

Travelling Supporters' Information:
Routes: From the East: Take the A723 into Merry Street and turn left into Brandon Street (1 mile). Follow through to Windmill Hill Street and turn right at the Fire Station into Knowetop Avenue for the ground; From Elsewhere: Exit the M74 at Junction 4 and take the A723 Hamilton Road into the Town Centre. Turn right into West Hamilton Street and follow into Brandon Street – then as from the East.

RANGERS FC

Founded: 1872 (**Entered League**: 1890)
Nickname: 'The Gers' 'Light Blues'
Ground: Ibrox Stadium, 150 Edmiston Drive, Glasgow   G51 2XD
Ground Capacity: 50,444 (All seats)
Record Attendance: 118,567 (2/1/39)
Pitch Size: 125 × 89 yards

Colours: Shirts are Blue with White collar and trim, White shorts
Telephone Nº: (0870) 600-1972
Ticket Office: (0870) 600-1993
Fax Number: (0870) 600-1978
Web Site: www.rangers.co.uk

GENERAL INFORMATION
Car Parking: Albion Car Park
Coach Parking: By Police direction
Nearest Railway Station: Ibrox (Underground) 2 mins. walk
Nearest Bus Station: Glasgow City Centre
Club Shop: The Rangers Superstore, Ibrox Stadium
Opening Times: Monday to Saturday 9.00am to 5.30pm; Sundays 11.00am to 5.00pm and also open one hour after the end of the game
Telephone Nº: (0141) 427-3710
Police Telephone Nº: (0141) 445-1113

GROUND INFORMATION
Away Supporters' Entrances & Sections:
Broomloan Road Turnstiles for Broomloan Road Stand

ADMISSION INFO (2006/2007 PRICES)
Adult Seating: £23.00 – £24.00
Child Seating: £12.00
Other Concessions: £12.00
Note: Most of the seats are taken by season-ticket holders
Programme Price: £2.00

DISABLED INFORMATION
Wheelchairs: 60 spaces for home fans, 5 for away fans in front of the West Enclosure
Helpers: Admitted
Prices: Free of charge for the disabled and helpers if they are members of the Disabled Supporters' Club
Disabled Toilets: Available in the West Enclosure
Contact: (0141) 580-8500   (Bookings are necessary)

Travelling Supporters' Information:
Routes: From All Parts: Exit the M8 at Junction 23. The road leads straight to the Stadium.

ST. MIRREN FC

Founded: 1877 (**Entered League**: 1890)
Nickname: 'The Saints' 'The Buddies'
Ground: St.Mirren Park, Love Street, Paisley, PA3 2EJ
Ground Capacity: 10,800 (all seats)
Record Attendance: 47,428 (7/3/25)
Pitch Size: 105 × 68 yards

Colours: Black and White striped shirts, White shorts
Telephone Nº: (0141) 889-2558
Ticket Line Nº: (0141) 840-4100
Fax Number: (0141) 848-6444
Web Site: www.saintmirren.net

GENERAL INFORMATION

Car Parking: Street parking
Coach Parking: Clark Street (off Greenock Road – 300 yards)
Nearest Railway Station: Paisley Gilmour Street (400 yards)
Nearest Bus Station: Paisley
Club Shop: Provan Sports, Causeyside Street, Paisley
Opening Times: Daily
Telephone Nº: (0141) 889-1629
Police Telephone Nº: (0141) 889-1113

GROUND INFORMATION

Away Supporters' Entrances & Sections:
Entrances on West of Main Stand for West Stand

ADMISSION INFO (2007/2008 PRICES)

Adult Seating: £18.00 – £22.00
Child/Concessionary Seating: £6.00 – £15.00
Note: Special Family Tickets are available and prices vary depending on the category of the game
Programme Price: £2.00

DISABLED INFORMATION

Wheelchairs: Accommodated in the West and East Stands
Helpers: Admitted
Prices: Free for the wheelchair disabled. Helpers £12.00
Disabled Toilets: 2 available in the West Stand
Contact: (0141) 840-1337 (Bookings are necessary)

Travelling Supporters' Information:
Routes: From All Parts: Exit the M8 at Junction 29 and take the A726 Greenock Road. The ground is approximately ½ mile along on the left – the floodlights make it clearly visible from some distance.

Also available from Soccer Books Ltd. –

A statistical record of football in Scotland featuring every League result and Final League table, Scottish Cup results from the Semi-finals onwards and lists of top goalscorers. ISBN 1-86223-123-0

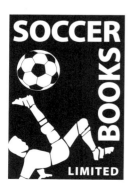

Softback Price £ 16.50

Available from all good book shops or order direct –

Soccer Books Limited
72 St. Peters Avenue
Cleethorpes
DN35 8HU
United Kingdom

Web site– www.soccer-books.co.uk

THE SCOTTISH FOOTBALL LEAGUE

Address   National Stadium, Hampden Park,
Mount Florida, Glasgow   G42 9BA

Founded   1890

Phone (0141) 620-4160   **Fax** (0141) 620-4161

Clubs for the 2007/2008 Season

AIRDRIE UNITED FC

Founded: 1965 (**Entered League**: 1966)
Former Name: Clydebank FC
Ground: Excelsior Stadium, Broomfield Park, Craigneuk Avenue, Airdrie   ML6 8QZ
Ground Capacity: 10,170 (All seats)
Record Attendance: 9,612

Pitch Size: 115 × 71 yards
Colours: White shirts with Red diamond, Red shorts
Telephone Nº: (07710) 230775
Ticket Office: (07710) 230775
Fax Number: (0141) 221-1497 or (01236) 626002
Web Site: www.airdrieunitedfc.com

GENERAL INFORMATION
Car Parking: Behind all the Stands
Coach Parking: Behind the East Stand
Nearest Railway Station: Drumgelloch (½ mile)
Nearest Bus Station: Gartlea – Airdrie Town Centre
Club Shop: At the ground
Opening Times: Opens at 12.00pm on Home Matchdays, every Friday 10.00am – 2.30pm & Sundays 2.00pm – 4.00pm
Telephone Nº: 07949 976116
Police Telephone Nº: (01236) 762222

GROUND INFORMATION
Away Supporters' Entrances & Sections:
East and South Stands

ADMISSION INFO (2007/2008 PRICES)
Adult Seating: £15.00
Child Seating: £7.00
Senior Citizen Seating: £10.00
Programme Price: £2.00

DISABLED INFORMATION
Wheelchairs: Spaces available for home and away fans accommodated in the front sections
Helpers: One admitted per disabled supporter
Prices: Disabled and helpers are admitted for half-price
Disabled Toilets: Available in all the stands
Contact: (07710) 230775   (Bookings are preferable)

Travelling Supporters' Information:
Routes: From the East: Exit the M8 at Junction 6 and take the A73 (signposted for Cumbernauld). Pass through Chapelhall into Airdrie and turn right into Petersburn Road – the ground is on the left; From the West: Take the A8 to the Chapelhall turn-off for Chapelhall. Join the A73 at Chapelhall, then as above.

ALBION ROVERS FC

Founded: 1882 (Entered League: 1903)
Nickname: 'Wee Rovers'
Ground: Cliftonhill Stadium, Main Street, Coatbridge,
Lanarkshire ML5 3RB
Ground Capacity: 1,238
Seating Capacity: 538
Record Attendance: 27,381 (8/2/36)

Pitch Size: 110 × 72 yards
Colours: Yellow and Blue shirts with Blue shorts
Telephone Nº: (01236) 606334
Ticket Office: (01236) 607041
Fax Number: (01236) 606334
Web Site: www.albionrovers.com

GENERAL INFORMATION

Car Parking: Street parking and Albion Street
Coach Parking: Street parking only
Nearest Railway Station: Coatdyke (10 minutes walk)
Nearest Bus Station: Coatbridge
Club Shop: At the ground
Opening Times: One hour before each home match
Telephone Nº: (01236) 606334
Police Telephone Nº: (01236) 502000

GROUND INFORMATION

Away Supporters' Entrances & Sections:
Main Street entrance for the Main Street Area

ADMISSION INFO (2007/2008 PRICES)

Adult Standing: £10.00
Adult Seating: £10.00
Student/Senior Citizen Standing/Seating: £5.00
Under-14s Standing/Seating: Free of charge
Programme Price: £1.00

DISABLED INFORMATION

Wheelchairs: Approximately 30 spaces available in the Disabled Area
Helpers: Please phone the club for information
Prices: Please phone the club for information
Disabled Toilets: Available at the East End of the Ground
Contact: (01236) 606334 (Bookings are preferred)

Travelling Supporters' Information:
Routes: From the East or West: Take the A8/M8 to the Shawhead Interchange then follow the A725 to the Town Centre. Follow A89 signs towards Airdrie at the roundabout, the ground is then on the left; From the South: Take the A725 from Bellshill/Hamilton/Motherwell/M74 to Coatbridge. Follow the A89 signs towards Airdrie at the roundabout, the ground is then on the left; From the North: Take the A73 to Airdrie then follow signs for the A8010 to Coatbridge. Join the A89 and the ground is one mile on the right.

ALLOA ATHLETIC FC

Founded: 1878 (**Entered League**: 1921)
Nickname: 'The Wasps'
Ground: Recreation Park, Clackmannan Road, Alloa, FK10 1RY
Ground Capacity: 3,100
Seating Capacity: 400
Record Attendance: 13,000 (26/2/39)

Pitch Size: 110 × 75 yards
Colours: Gold and Black shirts with Black shorts
Telephone Nº: (01259) 722695
Ticket Office: (01259) 722695
Fax Number: (01259) 210886
Web Site: www.alloaathletic.co.uk

GENERAL INFORMATION
Car Parking: A Car Park is adjacent to the ground
Coach Parking: By Police Direction
Nearest Railway Station: Stirling (7 miles)
Nearest Bus Station: Alloa
Club Shop: At the ground
Opening Times: Matchdays only 1.30pm to 5.00pm
Telephone Nº: (01259) 722695
Police Telephone Nº: (01259) 723255

GROUND INFORMATION
Away Supporters' Entrances & Sections:
Hilton Road entrance for the Hilton Road Side and
Clackmannan Road End

ADMISSION INFO (2007/2008 PRICES)
Adult Standing: £10.00
Adult Seating: £11.00
Senior Citizen/Child Standing: £5.00
Senior Citizen/Child Seating: £6.00
Programme Price: £1.50

DISABLED INFORMATION
Wheelchairs: Accommodated in the Disabled Section underneath the Main Stand
Helpers: Admitted
Prices: Free of charge for the disabled and helpers
Disabled Toilets: One available in the Main Stand
Contact: (01259) 722695 (Bookings are not necessary)

Travelling Supporters' Information:
Routes: From the South and East: Take the M74 to the M80 and exit at Junction 9 following the A907 into Alloa. Continue over two roundabouts passing the brewery and Town Centre. The Ground is on the left-hand side of the road.

ARBROATH FC

Founded: 1878 (**Entered League:** 1902)
Nickname: 'The Red Lichties'
Ground: Gayfield Park, Arbroath DD11 1QB
Ground Capacity: 4,153
Seating Capacity: 848
Record Attendance: 13,510 (23/2/52)

Pitch Size: 115 × 70 yards
Colours: Maroon and White shirts with Maroon shorts
Telephone Nº: (01241) 872157
Ticket Office: (01241) 872157
Fax Number: (01241) 431125
Web Site: www.arbroathfc.co.uk

GENERAL INFORMATION
Car Parking: Car Park in Queen's Drive
Coach Parking: Car Park in Queen's Drive
Nearest Railway Station: Arbroath (15 minutes walk)
Nearest Bus Station: Arbroath (10 minutes walk)
Club Shop: At the ground
Opening Times: Matchdays only 2.00pm – 5.00pm
Telephone Nº: (01241) 872838
Police Telephone Nº: (01241) 872222

GROUND INFORMATION
Away Supporters' Entrances & Sections:
Queen's Drive End

ADMISSION INFO (2007/2008 PRICES)
Adult Standing: £9.00
Adult Seating: £9.00
Concessionary Standing: £5.00
Concessionary Seating: £5.00
Family Ticket: 1 adult + 1 child £12.00
Programme Price: £1.50

DISABLED INFORMATION
Wheelchairs: 6 spaces available at both of the West and East Ends of the Main Stand
Helpers: Admitted
Prices: Normal prices for the disabled and helpers
Disabled Toilets: Two available at the rear of the Stand
Contact: (01241) 872157 (Bookings are not necessary)

Travelling Supporters' Information:
Routes: From Dundee and the West: Take the A92 (Coast Road). On entering Arbroath, pass under the Railway Line and the ground is on the right-hand side; From Stonehaven/Montrose: Take the A92, pass through Arbroath, go past the Harbour and the ground is on the left-hand side.

AYR UNITED FC

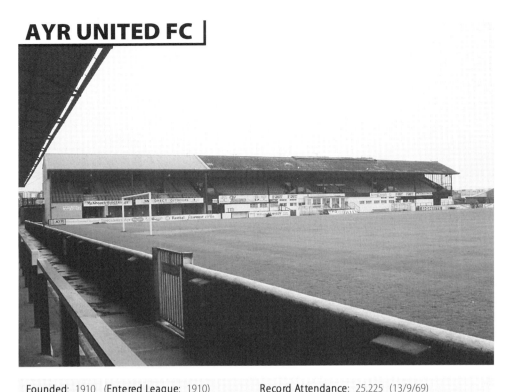

Founded: 1910 (**Entered League:** 1910)
Former Names: Formed by the amagamation of Ayr Parkhouse FC and Ayr FC in 1910
Nickname: 'The Honest Men'
Ground: Somerset Park, Tryfield Place, Ayr, KA8 9NB
Ground Capacity: 10,185
Seating Capacity: 1,500

Record Attendance: 25,225 (13/9/69)
Pitch Size: 110 × 72 yards
Colours: White shirts with Black shorts
Telephone Nº: (01292) 263435
Ticket Office: (01292) 263435
Fax Number: (01292) 281314
Web site: www.ayrunitedfc.co.uk

GENERAL INFORMATION

Car Parking: Craigie Car Park, Ayr Racecourse and Somerset Road Car Park
Coach Parking: Craigie Car Park
Nearest Railway Station: Ayr or Newton-on-Ayr (both stations are 10 minutes walk)
Nearest Bus Station: Sandgate, Ayr
Club Shop: At the ground
Opening Times: Monday to Friday and Matchdays 9.00am to 5.00pm
Telephone Nº: (01292) 263435
Police Telephone Nº: (01292) 664000

GROUND INFORMATION

Away Supporters' Entrances & Sections:
Turnstiles 1-7 for the Railway End (covered terrace) + turnstiles 9-10 for Main Stand accommodation

ADMISSION INFO (2007/2008 PRICES)

Adult Standing: £10.00
Adult Seating: £15.00
Child/Senior Citizen Standing: £5.00
Senior Citizen Seating: £10.00
Child Seating: In the Family Stand only – 1 Adult + 1 Child for £12.50 (each additional child is £5.00)
Programme Price: £2.00

DISABLED INFORMATION

Wheelchairs: 24 spaces are available in the Disabled Area beneath the Family Stand
Helpers: One admitted per wheelchair
Prices: Free for one wheelchair plus helper
Disabled Toilets: Available in the Disabled Area
Are Bookings Necessary: Only for all-ticket games
Contact: (01292) 263435

Travelling Supporters' Information:
Routes: Make for the A77 Ring Road around Ayr, exit via Whitletts Roundabout onto the A719 and follow the road towards Ayr. Just past the end of the racecourse, turn right at the traffic lights into Burnett Terrace, a sharp left and then right takes you into Somerset Road for the ground. (For car parking on Matchdays turn left at the traffic lights and then right 50 yards on into Craigie Park or on Somerset Road just past the ground on the left into Somerset Road car park).

BERWICK RANGERS FC

Founded: 1881 (**Entered League:** 1951)
Nickname: 'The Borderers'
Ground: Shielfield Park, Shielfield Terrace, Tweedmouth, Berwick-upon-Tweed   TD15 2EF
Ground Capacity: 4,131
Seating Capacity: 1,366
Record Attendance: 13,365 (28/1/67)

Pitch Size: 110 × 70 yards
Colours: Black and Gold striped shirts, Black shorts
Telephone Nº: (01289) 307424
Ticket Office: (01289) 307424
Fax Number: (01289) 309424
Web Site: www.berwickrangers.net

GENERAL INFORMATION

Car Parking: Large Car Park at the ground
Coach Parking: At the ground
Nearest Railway Station: Berwick-upon-Tweed (1½ miles)
Nearest Bus Station: Berwick Town Centre (1 mile)
Club Shop: Inside the Stadium
Opening Times: Matchdays Only (+ Mail order sales)
Telephone Nº: (01289) 307424
Police Telephone Nº: (01289) 307111

GROUND INFORMATION

Away Supporters' Entrances & Sections:
Shielfield Terrace entrance for the Popular Side Terrace (Gates A or B), Gate B for Main Stand accommodation. Gate A is only used for selected matches.

ADMISSION INFO (2007/2008 PRICES)

Adult Standing: £10.00
Adult Seating: £10.00
Concessions: £5.00
Schoolchildren: £2.00
Programme Price: £2.00

DISABLED INFORMATION

Wheelchairs: Accommodated in the Main Stand
Helpers: Admitted with wheelchair disabled
Prices: The disabled are admitted free of charge
Disabled Toilets: Available in the General Toilet Block and to the rear of the covered terracing.
Also available in the Black & Gold Pub by the car park
Contact: (01289) 307424/307623 (Bookings are necessary)

Travelling Supporters' Information:
Routes: From the North: Take the A1 (Berwick Bypass), cross the new road-bridge then take the 1st exit at the roundabout. Carry on for approximately ¼ mile to the next roundabout, go straight across then continue for approximately ¼ mile into Shielfield Terrace. Turn left and the ground is on the left; From the South: Take the A1 Bypass and continue across the first roundabout signposted Scremerston/Tweedmouth and then on for 1 mile. At the crossroads/junction take 'Spittal' Road (right) and continue for approximately 1 mile until the road becomes Shielfield Terrace. The ground is on the left in Shielfield Terrace.

BRECHIN CITY FC

Founded: 1906 (**Entered League**: 1923)
Nickname: 'The City'
Ground: Glebe Park, Trinity Road, Brechin, Angus, DD9 6BJ
Ground Capacity: 3,960
Seating Capacity: 1,519
Record Attendance: 9,123 (3rd February 1973)

Pitch Size: 110 × 67 yards
Colours: Red and White shirts and shorts
Telephone Nº: (01356) 622856
Ticket Office: (01356) 622856
Fax Number: (01356) 625667
Secretary's Number: 07810 226224
Web Site: www.brechincity.co.uk

GENERAL INFORMATION
Car Parking: Small Car Park at the ground and street parking
Coach Parking: Street parking
Nearest Railway Station: Montrose (8 miles)
Nearest Bus Station: Brechin
Club Shop: At the ground
Opening Times: Matchdays Only
Telephone Nº: (01356) 622856
Police Telephone Nº: (01356) 622222

GROUND INFORMATION
Away Supporters' Entrances & Sections:
Main Stand – Trinity Road End

ADMISSION INFO (2007/2008 PRICES)
Adult Standing: £12.00
Adult Seating: £12.00
Child Standing: £6.00
Child Seating: £6.00
Parent & Child Ticket: £15.00
Programme Price: £1.50

DISABLED INFORMATION
Wheelchairs: 10 spaces each for home and away fans
Helpers: Please phone the club for details
Prices: Please phone the club for details
Disabled Toilets: Two available in the Covered Enclosure
Contact: (01356) 622856   (Bookings are not necessary)

Travelling Supporters' Information:
Routes: From the South and West: Take the M90 to the A94 and continue along past the first 'Brechin' turn-off. Take the second turn signposted 'Brechin'. On entering Brechin, the ground is on the left-hand side of the road between some houses.

CLYDE FC

Founded: 1877 (**Entered League**: 1906)
Nickname: 'Bully Wee'
Ground: Broadwood Stadium, Cumbernauld, Glasgow   G68 9NE
Ground Capacity: 8,200 (all seats)
Record Attendance: 8,000 (14/8/96)
Pitch Size: 115 × 75 yards

Colours: White Shirts with Black piping, Black shorts
Telephone Nº: (01236) 451511
Ticket Office: (01236) 451511
Fax Number: (01236) 733490
Web Site: www.clydefc.co.uk

GENERAL INFORMATION
Car Parking: Behind the Main and West Stands
Coach Parking: Behind the Main Stand
Nearest Railway Station: Croy (1½ miles)
Nearest Bus Station: Cumbernauld Town Centre
Club Shop: At the ground
Opening Times: One hour before and after the match
Telephone Nº: (01236) 451511
Police Telephone Nº: (01236) 736085

GROUND INFORMATION
Away Supporters' Entrances & Sections:
West Stand Turnstile for the West Stand area

ADMISSION INFO (2007/2008 PRICES)
Adult Seating: £16.00
Child Seating: £6.00
Senior Citizen Seating: £8.00
Parent + 1 Child Seating: £17.00
Programme Price: £2.00

DISABLED INFORMATION
Wheelchairs: 10 spaces each for home and away fans accommodated in front sections of each stand
Helpers: One helper admitted per wheelchair
Prices: Free of charge for the disabled and helpers
Disabled Toilets: 4 available in the Main and West Stands
Contact: (01236) 451511   (Bookings are not necessary)

Travelling Supporters' Information:
Routes: From all Parts: Exit the A80 at Broadwood Junction and follow the signs for Broadwood. The ground is signposted from the next roundabout.

COWDENBEATH FC

Founded: 1881 (**Entered League**: 1905)
Nickname: 'Cowden' 'Blue Brazil'
Ground: Central Park, High Street, Cowdenbeath KY4 9QQ
Ground Capacity: 4,370
Seating Capacity: 1,431
Record Attendance: 25,586 (21/9/49)
Pitch Size: 107 × 64 yards

Colours: Shirts are Royal Blue with White trim, Shorts are White
Telephone Nº: (01383) 610166
Ticket Office: (01383) 610166
Fax Number: (01383) 512132
Web Site: www.cowdenbeathfc.com

GENERAL INFORMATION

Car Parking: Car Park at the ground and Stenhouse Street (200 yards). A total of 200 spaces are available
Coach Parking: King Street and Rowan Terrace
Nearest Railway Station: Cowdenbeath (400 yards)
Nearest Bus Station: Cowdenbeath (Bus Stop at ground)
Club Shop: At the ground
Opening Times: Weekdays 10.00am to 3.00pm; Saturdays 1.00pm to 3.00pm
Telephone Nº: (01383) 610166
Police Telephone Nº: (01383) 318600

GROUND INFORMATION

Away Supporters' Entrances & Sections:
Main Entrance for the South and East Sides

ADMISSION INFO (2007/2008 PRICES)

Adult Standing: £10.00
Adult Seating: £10.00
Child Standing: £5.00
Child Seating: £5.00
Programme Price: £1.00

DISABLED INFORMATION

Wheelchairs: 3 spaces each for home and away fans
Helpers: Please phone the club for information
Prices: Please phone the club for information
Disabled Toilets: 1 Ladies, 1 Gents and 1 Unisex available
Contact: (01383) 610166 (Bookings are necessary)

Travelling Supporters' Information:
Routes: Exit the M90 at Junction 3 for Dunfermline. Take the Dual Carriageway to Cowdenbeath and follow straight on into the High Street. The ground is situated on the first left turn in the High Street.

DUMBARTON FC

Founded: 1872 (**Entered League**: 1890)
Nickname: 'Sons'
Ground: Strathclyde Homes Stadium, Castle Road, Dumbarton G82 1JJ
Ground Capacity: 2,046 (All seats)
Record Attendance: 2,035 (27th January 2001)

Pitch Size: 110 × 72 yards
Colours: Shirts are Gold with Black Trim, Black shorts
Telephone Nº: (01389) 762569
Ticket Office: (01389) 762569
Fax Number: (01389) 762629
Web Site: www.dumbartonfootballclub.com

GENERAL INFORMATION

Car Parking: 400 spaces available at the ground
Coach Parking: At the ground
Nearest Railway Station: Dumbarton East
Nearest Bus Station: Dumbarton
Club Shop: At the ground
Opening Times: Weekdays and Saturday matchdays 9.00am to 3.00pm
Telephone Nº: (01389) 762569
Police Telephone Nº: (01389) 822000

GROUND INFORMATION

Away Supporters' Entrances & Sections:
West Section

ADMISSION INFO (2007/2008 PRICES)

Adult Seating: £11.00
Child Seating: £6.00
Programme Price: £1.50

DISABLED INFORMATION

Wheelchairs: Approximately 24 spaces available in the disabled area
Helpers: Please phone the club for information
Prices: Please phone the club for information
Disabled Toilets: Available
Contact: (01389) 762569 (Bookings are necessary)

Travelling Supporters' Information:
Routes: The ground is situated just by Dumbarton Castle. Take the A814 into Dumbarton and follow the brown signs for the Castle to find the ground.

DUNDEE FC

Founded: 1893   (**Entered League**: 1893)
Nickname: 'The Dee'
Ground: Dens Park Stadium, Sandeman Street, Dundee   DD3 7JY
Ground Capacity: 11,850   (All seats)
Record Attendance: 43,024 (7/2/53)

Pitch Size: 105 × 70 yards
Colours: Blue shirts with White shorts
Telephone N°: (01382) 889966
Ticket Office: (01382) 889966
Fax Number: (01382) 832284
Web Site: www.thedees.co.uk

GENERAL INFORMATION

Car Parking: Street parking only
Coach Parking: Please contact the club for details
Nearest Railway Station: Dundee
Nearest Bus Station: Dundee
Club Shop: Commercial Street, Dundee
Opening Times: Weekdays from 9.00am to 5.00pm
Telephone N°: (01382) 889966
Police Telephone N°: (01382) 223200

GROUND INFORMATION

Away Supporters' Entrances & Sections:
Turnstiles 33-38 for East Stand accommodation

ADMISSION INFO (2007/2008 PRICES)

Adult Seating: £16.00
Child Seating: £8.00
Senior Citizen Seating: £8.00
Note: Higher prices are charged for matches against Celtic, Rangers and Dundee United. Reduced prices for children are available in the Family Stand
Programme Price: £2.00

DISABLED INFORMATION

Wheelchairs: Accommodated in the East and West Stands
Helpers: Admitted free of charge
Prices: £5.00 for the disabled in the Disabled Area only
Disabled Toilets: Adjacent to the Disabled Area
Contact: (01382) 889966   (Bookings are necessary)

Travelling Supporters' Information:
Routes: Take the A972 from Perth (Kingsway West) to King's Cross Circus Roundabout. Take the 3rd exit into Clepington Road and turn right into Provost Road for 1 mile then take the 2nd left into Sandeman Street for the ground.

DUNFERMLINE ATHLETIC FC

Founded: 1885 (**Entered League**: 1921)
Nickname: 'The Pars'
Ground: East End Park, Halbeath Road, Dunfermline, Fife, KY12 7RB
Ground Capacity: 11,780 (All seats)
Record Attendance: 27,816 (30/4/68)

Pitch Size: 115 × 71 yards
Colours: Black and White shirts and shorts
Telephone Nº: (01383) 724295
Ticket Office: 0870 300-1201
Fax Number: (01383) 626452
Web Site: www.dafc.co.uk

GENERAL INFORMATION

Car Parking: Limited spaces in a Car Park at the ground. Otherwise, a Multistorey Car Park is 10 minutes walk
Coach Parking: Leys Park Road
Nearest Railway Station: Dunfermline Queen Margaret (10 minutes walk)
Nearest Bus Station: East Port, Dunfermline (10 minutes walk)
Club Shop: 18 Guildhall Street, Dunfermline
Opening Times: Monday to Saturday 9.00am – 5.30pm
Telephone Nº: (01383) 626737
Police Telephone Nº: (01383) 318700

GROUND INFORMATION

Away Supporters' Entrances & Sections:
Turnstiles 10-15 for the East Stand. Turnstiles 16-18 for the North East Stand

ADMISSION INFO (2007/2008 PRICES)

Adult Seating: £16.00 – £18.00
Under-16s/Other Concessions Seating: £10.00 – £12.00
Under-12s Seating: £5.00 – £7.00
Note: Match prices vary according to the category of game
Programme Price: £2.50

DISABLED INFORMATION

Wheelchairs: 12 spaces each for home & away fans
Helpers: One admitted per wheelchair
Prices: Concessionary prices for the wheelchair disabled. Helpers are admitted free of charge
Disabled Toilets: Available in West and East Stands and also in the Main Stand Hospitality Area
Contact: 0870 300-1201 (Bookings are necessary)

Travelling Supporters' Information:
Routes: From the Forth Road Bridge and Perth: Exit the M90 at Junction 3 and take the A907 (Halbeath Road) into Dunfermline – the ground is on right; From Kincardine Bridge and Alloa: Take the A985 to the A994 into Dunfermline. Take Pittencrief Street, Glen Bridge and Carnegie Drive to Sinclair Gardens roundabout. Take the 1st exit toward the Traffic Lights then turn right into Ley's Park Road. Take the second exit on the right into the Car Park at the rear of the stadium.

EAST FIFE FC

Founded: 1903 (**Entered League:** 1903)
Nickname: 'The Fife'
Ground: First 2 Finance Bayview Stadium,
Harbour View, Methil, Fife   KY8 3RW
Ground Capacity: 2,000 (All seats)
Record Attendance: 22,515 (2/1/50)

Pitch Size: 113 × 73 yards
Colours: Black and Gold striped shirts, Black shorts
Telephone N°: (01333) 426323
Ticket Office: (01333) 426323
Fax Number: (01333) 426376
Web Site: www.eastfife.org

GENERAL INFORMATION

Car Parking: Adjacent to the ground
Coach Parking: Adjacent to the ground
Nearest Railway Station: Kirkcaldy (8 miles)
Nearest Bus Station: Leven
Club Shop: At the ground
Opening Times: Matchdays and normal office hours
Telephone N°: (01333) 426323
Police Telephone N°: (01592) 418900

GROUND INFORMATION

Away Supporters' Entrances & Sections:
Accommodated within the Main Stand

ADMISSION INFO (2007/2008 PRICES)

Adult Seating: £10.00
Child Seating: £5.00
Programme Price: £2.00

DISABLED INFORMATION

Wheelchairs: 24 spaces available in total
Helpers: Admitted
Prices: Normal prices charged for the disabled and helpers
Disabled Toilets: Yes
Contact: (01333) 426323   (Bookings are necessary)

Travelling Supporters' Information:
Routes: Take the A915 from Kirkcaldy past Buckhaven and Methil to Leven. Turn right at the traffic lights and go straight on at the first roundabout then turn right at the second roundabout. Cross Bawbee Bridge and turn left at the next roundabout. The ground is the first turning on the left after ¼ mile.

EAST STIRLINGSHIRE FC

Founded: 1881 (**Entered League**: 1900)
Former Names: Bainsford Britannia FC
Nickname: 'The Shire'
Ground: Firs Park, Firs Street, Falkirk   FK2 7AY
Ground Capacity: 536
Seating Capacity: 280
Record Attendance: 12,000 (21/2/21)

Pitch Size: 110 × 71 yards
Colours: All White shirts and shorts
Telephone Nº: (01324) 623583
Ticket Office: (01324) 623583
Fax Number: (01324) 637862
Web Site: www.eaststirlingfc.co.uk

GENERAL INFORMATION
Car Parking: Street parking
Coach Parking: Street parking
Nearest Railway Station: Grahamston (10 minutes walk)
Nearest Bus Station: Falkirk
Club Shop: At the ground
Opening Times: Weekdays (except Wednesdays) and Saturday Matchdays 10.00am to 12.00pm
Telephone Nº: (01324) 623583
Police Telephone Nº: (01324) 634212

GROUND INFORMATION
Away Supporters' Entrances & Sections:
No usual segregation

ADMISSION INFO (2007/2008 PRICES)
Adult Standing: £9.00
Adult Seating: £9.00
Child/Senior Citizen Standing: £4.50
Child/Senior Citizen Seating: £4.50
Programme Price: £1.50

DISABLED INFORMATION
Wheelchairs: Accommodated
Helpers: Admitted
Prices: £2.50 each for both disabled and helpers
Disabled Toilets: Available in the Main Stand
Contact: (01324) 623583   (Bookings are necessary)

Travelling Supporters' Information:
Routes: From Glasgow and Edinburgh: Exit the Motorway at signs marked Grangemouth. Follow the AA signs for football traffic into Falkirk as far as Thornhill Road (where the road meets the 'Give Way' sign). Once in Thornhill Road turn left into Firs Street at St. James' Church. The ground is straight ahead.

ELGIN CITY FC

Founded: 1893 **(Entered League:** 2000)
Nickname: 'Black and Whites'
Ground: Borough Briggs, Borough Briggs Road, Elgin   IV30 1AP
Ground Capacity: 3,900
Seating Capacity: 478
Record Attendance: 12,640 (17/2/68)

Pitch Size: 120 × 86 yards
Colours: Black and White shirts with Black shorts
Telephone Nº: (01343) 551114
Ticket Information: (01343) 551114
Fax Number: (01343) 547921
Web Site: www.elgincity.com (Unofficial site)

GENERAL INFORMATION

Car Parking: At the ground
Coach Parking: At the ground
Nearest Railway Station: Elgin (1 mile)
Nearest Bus Station: Elgin (¼ mile)
Club Shop: At the ground
Opening Times: Weekdays 9.30am to 4.30pm and also Saturdays 10.00am to 5.00pm (home matchdays only)
Telephone Nº: (01343) 551114
Police Telephone Nº: (01343) 543101

GROUND INFORMATION

Away Supporters' Entrances & Sections:
West End entrances for the Covered Enclosure

ADMISSION INFO (2007/2008 PRICES)

Adult Standing: £9.00
Adult Seating: £11.00
Child Standing: £4.00
Child Seating: £6.00
Programme Price: £1.50

DISABLED INFORMATION

Wheelchairs: Accommodated
Helpers: Admitted
Prices: The disabled are admitted at concessionary prices
Disabled Toilets: Available
Contact: (01343) 551114   (Bookings are not necessary)

Travelling Supporters' Information:
Routes: Take the Alexandra bypass to the roundabout ½ mile from the City Centre and turn left towards Lossiemouth. Borough Briggs Road is on the left.

FORFAR ATHLETIC FC

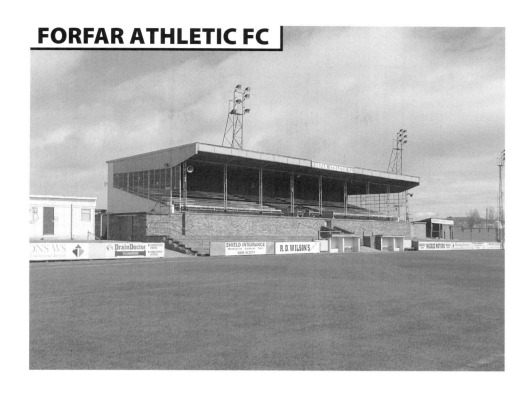

Founded: 1885 (**Entered League:** 1921)
Nickname: 'Loons'
Ground: Station Park, Carseview Road, Forfar, Angus   DD8 3BT
Ground Capacity: 4,602
Seating Capacity: 739
Record Attendance: 10,780 (2/2/70)

Pitch Size: 115 × 69 yards
Colours: Sky Blue shirts with Navy trim, Navy shorts
Telephone Nº: (01307) 463576
Ticket Office: (01307) 463576
Fax Number: (01307) 466956
Web Site: www.forfarathletic.co.uk

GENERAL INFORMATION
Car Parking: Market Muir Car Park and adjacent streets
Coach Parking: Market Muir Car Park
Nearest Railway Station: Dundee or Arbroath (14 miles)
Nearest Bus Station: Forfar (½ mile)
Club Shop: None
Police Telephone Nº: (01307) 462551

GROUND INFORMATION
Away Supporters' Entrances & Sections:
West End entrances for West End Terracing and North part of the Main Stand

ADMISSION INFO (2006/2007 PRICES)
Adult Standing: £10.00
Adult Seating: £10.50
Child Standing: £5.00
Child Seating: £5.50
Programme Price: £1.00

DISABLED INFORMATION
Wheelchairs: 4 spaces each for home and away fans accommodated to the west of the Main Stand
Helpers: Please phone the club for details
Prices: Please phone the club for details
Disabled Toilets: One available
Contact: (01307) 463576   (Bookings are necessary)

Travelling Supporters' Information:
Routes: Take the A85/M90 to Dundee and then the A929. Exit at the 2nd turn-off (signposted for Forfar). On the outskirts of Forfar, turn right at the T-junction and then left at the next major road. The ground is signposted on the left (down the cobbled street with the railway arch).

GREENOCK MORTON FC

Founded: 1874 (**Entered League**: 1893)
Nickname: 'Ton'
Ground: Cappielow Park, Sinclair Street, Greenock, PA15 2TY
Ground Capacity: 11,589
Seating Capacity: 6,039
Record Attendance: 23,500 (29/4/21)

Pitch Size: 110 × 71 yards
Colours: Blue and White hooped shirts, Blue shorts
Telephone Nº: (01475) 723571
Ticket Office: (01475) 723571
Fax Number: (01475) 781084
Web Site: www.gmfc.net

GENERAL INFORMATION

Car Parking: At the ground (£2.00 fee) or Street parking
Coach Parking: James Watt Dock
Nearest Railway Station: Cartsdyke (½ mile)
Nearest Bus Station: Town Centre (1½ miles)
Club Shop: At the ground
Opening Times: Weekdays 12.00pm to 4.00pm. Saturday matchdays open before and after the match
Telephone Nº: (01475) 723571 Ext. 28
Fax Nº: (01475) 781084
Police Telephone Nº: (01475) 492500

GROUND INFORMATION

Away Supporters' Entrances & Sections:
East Hamilton Street turnstiles

ADMISSION INFO (2007/2008 PRICES)

Adult Standing: £11.00
Adult Seating: £13.00
Under-16s Standing: £3.00
Parent & Child Seating: £15.00
Senior Citizen Standing: £6.00
Senior Citizen Seating: £7.00
Programme Price: £1.50

DISABLED INFORMATION

Wheelchairs: 5 spaces each for home and away fans accommodated below the Grandstand
Helpers: One helper admitted per disabled fan
Prices: Free of charge for the disabled and helpers
Disabled Toilets: One available
Contact: (01475) 723571 (Bookings are necessary)

Travelling Supporters' Information:
Routes: From the North: Take the M8 to the A8. From Port Glasgow follow the A78 to Greenock. Cappielow Park is on the left after passing under the railway bridge; From the South: Take the A78 to Greenock. Follow the road past IBM then turn right at the second set of lights into Dunlop Street. Follow this road until it turns sharp left and goes downhill and continue to the traffic lights facing the river. Turn right onto the A8, cross two roundabouts and Cappielow Park is on the right hand side of the road.

HAMILTON ACADEMICAL FC

Founded: 1874 (**Entered League**: 1897)
Nickname: 'The Accies'
Ground: New Douglas Park, Cadzow Avenue,
Hamilton   ML3 0FT
Ground Capacity: 5,536 (all seats)
Record Attendance: 4,975 (at New Douglas Park)

Pitch Size: 115 × 75 yards
Colours: Red and White hooped shirts, shorts are
White with a Red flash
Telephone Nº: (01698) 368650
Fax Number: (01698) 285422
Web Site: www.acciesfc.co.uk

GENERAL INFORMATION

Car Parking: At the ground and in the adjacent Caird Street
Council Car Park
Coach Parking: In the Caird Street Car Park
Nearest Railway Station: Hamilton West (200 yards)
Nearest Bus Station: Hamilton (1 mile)
Club Shop: At the Stadium
Opening Times: Monday, Tuesday, Thursday, Friday and
Saturday Matchdays 10.00am to 6.00pm
Telephone Nº: None
Police Telephone Nº: (01698) 483300

GROUND INFORMATION

Away Supporters' Entrances & Sections:
North Stand – use turnstiles 7 to 12

ADMISSION INFO (2007/2008 PRICES)

Adult Seating: £14.00
Child/Senior Citizen Seating: £6.00
Programme Price: £1.50

DISABLED INFORMATION

Wheelchairs: Accommodated in the front row of the stand
or by the trackside
Helpers: Admitted following prior booking
Prices: Free for the disabled and one helper
Disabled Toilets: Available
Contact: (01698) 368650   (Bookings are necessary)

Travelling Supporters' Information:
Routes: Exit the M74 at Junction 5 and follow signs marked "Football Traffic". Go past Hamilton Racecourse, turn right at the lights by Hamilton Business Park then first right again for New Park Street and Auchinraith Avenue. The ground is behind Morrisons and Sainsburys.

LIVINGSTON FC

Founded: 1943 (**Entered League**: 1974)
Former Names: Ferranti Thistle FC, Meadowbank Thistle FC
Nickname: 'The Lions'
Ground: Almondvale Stadium, Alderstone Road, Livingston   EH54 7DN
Ground Capacity: 10,006 (All seats)

Record Attendance: 10,006 (vs Rangers)
Pitch Size: 105 × 72 yards
Colours: Gold shirts and shorts
Telephone Nº: (01506) 417000
Ticket Office: (01506) 471000
Fax Number: (01506) 418888
Web Site: www.livingstonfc.co.uk

GENERAL INFORMATION
Car Parking: Car Park at the ground by arrangement
Coach Parking: At the ground
Nearest Railway Station: Livingston
Nearest Bus Station: Livingston
Club Shop: At the Stadium
Opening Times: Daily – please phone for further details
Police Telephone Nº: (01506) 431200

GROUND INFORMATION
Away Supporters' Entrances & Sections:
East Stand entrances and accommodation

ADMISSION INFO (2007/2008 PRICES)
Adult Seating: £18.00
Child Seating: £7.00
Programme Price: £2.50

DISABLED INFORMATION
Wheelchairs: Accommodated
Helpers: Please phone the club for information
Prices: Please phone the club for information
Disabled Toilets: Available
Contact: (01506) 417000   (Bookings are necessary)

Travelling Supporters' Information:
Routes: Exit the M8 at the Livingston turn-off and take the A899 to the Cousland Interchange. Turn right into Cousland Road, pass the Hospital, then turn left into Alderstone Road and the stadium is on the left opposite the Campus.

MONTROSE FC

Founded: 1879 (**Entered League**: 1929)
Nickname: 'Gable Endies'
Ground: Links Park Stadium, Wellington Street,
Montrose   DD10 8QD
Ground Capacity: 3,292
Seating Capacity: 1,338
Record Attendance: 8,983 (vs Dundee – 17/3/73)

Pitch Size: 113 × 70 yards
Colours: Royal Blue shirts with Blue shorts
Telephone Nº: (01674) 673200
Ticket Office: (01674) 673200
Fax Number: (01674) 677311
Web Site: www.montrosefc.co.uk

GENERAL INFORMATION
Car Parking: At the ground and Street parking also
Coach Parking: Mid-Links
Nearest Railway Station: Montrose Western Road
Nearest Bus Station: High Street, Montrose
Club Shop: At the ground
Opening Times: Weekdays 10.00am to 3.00pm
Telephone Nº: (01674) 673200
Police Telephone Nº: (01674) 672222

GROUND INFORMATION
Away Supporters' Entrances & Sections:
No usual segregation

ADMISSION INFO (2006/2007 PRICES)
Adult Standing: £9.00
Adult Seating: £9.00
Child Standing: £4.50
Child Seating: £4.50
Programme Price: £1.50

DISABLED INFORMATION
Wheelchairs: 5 spaces available in the Main Stand
Helpers: Please phone the club for information
Prices: Please phone the club for information
Disabled Toilets: 2 available in the Main Stand
Contact: (01674) 673200   (Bookings are helpful)

Travelling Supporters' Information:
Routes: Take the main A92 Coastal Road to Montrose. Once in the town, the ground is well signposted and is situated in the
Mid-Links area.

PARTICK THISTLE FC

Founded: 1876 (**Entered League**: 1890)
Nickname: 'The Jags'
Ground: Firhill Stadium, 80 Firhill Road, Glasgow, G20 7AL
Ground Capacity: 10,921 (All seats)
Record Attendance: 49,838 (18/2/22)
Pitch Size: 110 × 75 yards

Colours: Red and Yellow striped shirts, Black shorts
Telephone Nº: (0141) 579-1971
Ticket Office: (0141) 579-1971
Fax Number: (0141) 945-1525
Web Site: www.ptfc.co.uk
e-mail: mail@ptfc.co.uk

GENERAL INFORMATION
Car Parking: Street parking
Coach Parking: Panmure Street
Nearest Railway Station: Maryhill
Nearest Underground Station: St. George's Cross
Club Shops: At the Stadium
Opening Times: Matchdays 12.00pm to 5.00pm or 5.30pm to 9.30pm for Night matches. A shop in the Office is open on Weekdays from 9.00am to 4.30pm
Telephone Nº: (0141) 579-1971
Police Telephone Nº: (0141) 532-3864

GROUND INFORMATION
Away Supporters' Entrances & Sections:
North Stand (enter via Firhill Road turnstiles)

ADMISSION INFO (2007/2008 PRICES)
Adult Seating: £15.00
Senior Citizen/Student Seating: £10.00
Under-16s Seating: £5.00
Programme Price: £2.00

DISABLED INFORMATION
Wheelchairs: 17 spaces in the North Enclosure
Helpers: One helper admitted per wheelchair
Prices: Free for the disabled and one helper
Disabled Toilets: Available in the North Enclosure and the North Stand
Contact: (0141) 579-1971 – Antonia Kerr
(Bookings are necessary)

Travelling Supporters' Information:
Routes: From the East: Exit the M8 at Junction 16; From the West: Exit the M8 at Junction 17. From both directions, follow Maryhill Road to Queen's Cross and the ground is on the right.

PETERHEAD FC

Founded: 1891   (**Entered League**: 2000)
Nickname: 'Blue Toon'
Ground: Balmoor Stadium, Peterhead   AB42 1EU
Ground Capacity: 3,300
Seating Capacity: 980
Record Attendance: 2,300
Pitch Size: 110 × 70 yards
Colours: Shirts and Shorts are Royal Blue with White piping

Telephone Nº: (01779) 478256
Fax Number: (01779) 490682
Contact Address: G.Moore, 23 Willowbank Road, Peterhead   AB42 2FG
Contact Phone Nº: (01779) 476870 (Home) or (01224) 820851 (Work)
Web Site: www.peterheadfc.org.uk

GENERAL INFORMATION

Car Parking: At the ground
Coach Parking: At the ground
Nearest Railway Station: Aberdeen
Nearest Bus Station: Peterhead
Club Shop: At the ground
Opening Times: Monday to Saturday 9.00am to 5.00pm
Telephone Nº: (01779) 478256
Police Telephone Nº: (01779) 472571

GROUND INFORMATION

Away Supporters' Entrances & Sections:
Segregation only used when required which is very rare

ADMISSION INFO (2006/2007 PRICES)

Adult Standing: £10.00
Adult Seating: £10.00
Child Standing: £5.00
Child Seating: £5.00
Programme Price: £1.50

DISABLED INFORMATION

Wheelchairs: Accommodated
Helpers: Please phone the club for details
Prices: Please phone the club for details
Disabled Toilets: Available
Contact: (01779) 473434   (Bookings are necessary)

Travelling Supporters' Information:
Routes: The ground is situated on the left of the main road from Fraserburgh (A952), 300 yards past the swimming pool.

QUEEN OF THE SOUTH FC

Founded: 1919 (**Entered League**: 1923)
Nickname: 'The Doonhamers'
Ground: Palmerston Park, Terregles Street, Dumfries, DG2 9BA
Ground Capacity: 6,412
Seating Capacity: 3,509
Record Attendance: 26,552 (23/2/52)

Pitch Size: 112 × 73 yards
Colours: Blue shirts with White shorts
Telephone Nº: (01387) 254853
Ticket Office: (01387) 254853
Fax Number: (01387) 240470
Web Site: www.qosfc.com

GENERAL INFORMATION
Car Parking: Car Park adjacent to the ground
Coach Parking: Car Park adjacent to the ground
Nearest Railway Station: Dumfries (¾ mile)
Nearest Bus Station: Dumfries Whitesands (5 minutes walk)
Club Shop: At the ground
Opening Times: Daily
Telephone Nº: (01387) 254853
Police Telephone Nº: (01387) 252112

GROUND INFORMATION
Away Supporters' Entrances & Sections:
Terregles Street entrances for the East Stand

ADMISSION INFO (2007/2008 PRICES)
Adult Standing: £15.00
Adult Seating: £15.00
Senior Citizen Standing/Seating: £6.00
Child Standing/Seating: £3.00
Programme Price: £2.00

DISABLED INFORMATION
Wheelchairs: Accommodated in front of the East Stand
Helpers: Admitted
Prices: £6.00 for the disabled, free of charge for helpers
Disabled Toilets: One available in the East Stand
Contact: (01387) 254853   (Bookings are necessary)

Travelling Supporters' Information:
Routes: From the East: Take the A75 to Dumfries and follow the ring road over the River Nith. Turn left at the 1st roundabout then right at the 2nd roundabout (the Kilmarnock/Glasgow Road roundabout). The ground is a short way along past the Tesco store; From the West: Take the A75 to Dumfries and proceed along ring road to the 1st roundabout (Kilmarnock/Glasgow Road) then as from the East; From the North: Take A76 to Dumfries and carry straight across 1st roundabout for the ground.

QUEEN'S PARK FC

Founded: 1867 (**Entered League**: 1900)
Nickname: 'The Spiders'
Ground: Hampden Park, Mount Florida, Glasgow, G42 9BA
Ground Capacity: 52,000 (All seats)
Record Attendance: 150,239 (17/4/37)

Pitch Size: 115 × 75 yards
Colours: Black and White hooped shirts, White shorts
Telephone Nº: (0141) 632-1275
Ticket Office: (0141) 632-1275
Fax Number: (0141) 636-1612
Web Site: www.queensparkfc.co.uk

GENERAL INFORMATION

Car Parking: Car Park at the Stadium
Coach Parking: Car Park at the Stadium
Nearest Railway Station: Mount Florida and King's Park (both 5 minutes walk)
Nearest Bus Station: Buchanan Street
Club Shop: At the ground
Opening Times: During home matches only
Telephone Nº: (0141) 632-1275
Police Telephone Nº: (0141) 532-4900

GROUND INFORMATION

Away Supporters' Entrances & Sections: South Stand

ADMISSION INFO (2007/2008 PRICES)

Adult Seating: £10.00
Concessionary Seating: £2.00
Family Ticket: £10.00 for a parent and then an extra £1.00 for each additional child after that
Programme Price: £2.00
Note: Only the South Stand is presently used for games

DISABLED INFORMATION

Wheelchairs: 160 spaces available in total
Helpers: Admitted
Prices: Free for the disabled. Helpers normal prices
Disabled Toilets: Available
Contact: (0141) 632-1275 (Bookings are necessary)

Travelling Supporters' Information:
Routes: From the South: Take the A724 to the Cambuslang Road and at Eastfield branch left into Main Street and follow through Burnhill Street and Westmuir Place into Prospecthill Road. Turn left into Aikenhead Road and right into Mount Annan for Kinghorn Drive and the Stadium; From the South: Take the A77 Fenwick Road, through Kilmarnock Road into Pollokshaws Road then turn right into Langside Avenue. Pass through Battle Place to Battlefield Road and turn left into Cathcart Road. Turn right into Letherby Drive, right into Carmunnock Road and 1st left into Mount Annan Drive for the Stadium; From the North & East: Exit M8 Junction 15 and passing Infirmary on left proceed into High Street and cross the Albert Bridge into Crown Street. Join Cathcart Road and proceed South until it becomes Carmunnock Road. Turn left into Mount Annan Drive and left again into Kinghorn Drive for the Stadium.

RAITH ROVERS FC

Founded: 1883 (**Entered League**: 1902)
Nickname: 'The Rovers'
Ground: Stark's Park, Pratt Street, Kirkcaldy, KY1 1SA
Ground Capacity: 10,104 (All seats)
Record Attendance: 31,306 (7/2/53)
Pitch Size: 113 × 70 yards

Colours: Navy Blue shirts with White shoulder panels, Navy Blue shorts with White trim
Telephone N°: (01592) 263514
Ticket Office: (01592) 263514
Fax Number: (01592) 642833
Web Site: www.raithroversfc.com

GENERAL INFORMATION
Car Parking: Esplanade and Beveridge Car Park
Coach Parking: Railway Station & Esplanade
Nearest Railway Station: Kirkcaldy (15 minutes walk)
Nearest Bus Station: Kirkcaldy (15 minutes walk)
Club Shop: At the ground
Opening Times: Matchdays only
Telephone N°: (01592) 263514
Police Telephone N°: (01592) 418700

GROUND INFORMATION
Away Supporters' Entrances & Sections:
North Stand and part of the Railway Stand

ADMISSION INFO (2007/2008 PRICES)
Adult Seating: £14.00
Senior Citizen/Child Seating: £7.00
Note: One adult and one child are admitted for £17.00
Programme Price: £2.00

DISABLED INFORMATION
Wheelchairs: 12 spaces each for home and away fans accommodated in the North & South Stands
Helpers: One helper admitted per wheelchair
Prices: Free of charge for the helpers. Disabled pay concessionary prices
Disabled Toilets: Available in the North and South Stands
Are Bookings Necessary: Only for all-ticket games
Contact: (01592) 263514

Travelling Supporters' Information:
Routes: Take the M8 to the end then follow the A90/M90 over the Forth Road Bridge. Exit the M90 at Junction 1 and follow the A921 to Kirkcaldy. On the outskirts of town, turn left at the B & Q roundabout from which the floodlights can be seen. The ground is raised on the hill nearby.

ROSS COUNTY FC

Founded: 1929 (**Entered League**: 1994)
Nickname: 'The County'
Ground: Victoria Park, Dingwall, Ross-shire, IV15 9QW
Ground Capacity: 6,500
Seating Capacity: 2,666
Record Attendance: 10,000 (19/2/66)

Pitch Size: 115 × 74 yards
Colours: Navy Blue shirts with White shorts
Telephone Nº: (01349) 860860
Ticket Office: (01349) 860860
Fax Number: (01349) 866277
Web Site: www.rosscountyfootballclub.co.uk

GENERAL INFORMATION
Car Parking: At the ground
Coach Parking: At the ground
Nearest Railway Station: Dingwall (adjacent)
Nearest Bus Station: Dingwall
Club Shop: At the ground
Opening Times: Weekdays and Matchdays
Telephone Nº: (01349) 860860
Police Telephone Nº: (01349) 862444

GROUND INFORMATION
Away Supporters' Entrances & Sections:
West Stand entrances and accommodation

ADMISSION INFO (2007/2008 PRICES)
Adult Standing: £10.00
Adult Seating: £12.00
Child Standing: £5.00
Child Seating: £6.00
Note: Family tickets are also available – prices on request
Programme Price: £2.00

DISABLED INFORMATION
Wheelchairs: 6 spaces each for home and away fans
Helpers: Admitted
Prices: Normal prices are charged
Disabled Toilets: Available at the bottom of the West Stand
Contact: (01349) 860860   (Bookings are necessary)

Travelling Supporters' Information:
Routes: The ground is situated at Dingwall adjacent to the Railway Station which is down Jubilee Park Road at the bottom of the High Street.

ST. JOHNSTONE FC

Founded: 1884 (**Entered League**: 1911)
Nickname: 'Saints'
Ground: McDiarmid Park, Crieff Road, Perth, PH1 2SJ
Ground Capacity: 10,721 (All seats)
Record Attendance: 10,545 (23/5/99)
Pitch Size: 115 × 75 yards

Colours: Blue shirts with White shorts
Telephone Nº: (01738) 459090
Ticket Office: (01738) 455000
Fax Number: (01738) 625771
Web Site: www.stjohnstonefc.co.uk

GENERAL INFORMATION

Car Parking: Car park at the ground
Coach Parking: At the ground
Nearest Railway Station: Perth (3 miles)
Nearest Bus Station: Perth (3 miles)
Club Shop: At the ground
Opening Times: Weekdays from 9.00am to 5.00pm and Matchdays 1.30pm to 3.00pm
Telephone Nº: (01738) 459090
Police Telephone Nº: (01738) 621141

GROUND INFORMATION

Away Supporters' Entrances & Sections:
North Stand and North End of the West Stand as necessary

ADMISSION INFO (2007/2008 PRICES)

Adult Seating: £17.00 – £19.00
Child Seating: £6.00 – £10.00
Other Concessions: £5.00 – £10.00
Programme Price: £2.50

DISABLED INFORMATION

Wheelchairs: 10 spaces each available for home and away fans in the East and West Stands
Helpers: Please phone the club for details
Prices: Please phone the club for details
Disabled Toilets: Available in the East and West Stands
Contact: (01738) 459090 (Bookings are necessary)

Travelling Supporters' Information:
Routes: Follow the M80 to Stirling, take the A9 Inverness Road north from Perth and follow the signs for the 'Football Stadium'. The ground is situated beside a dual-carriageway – the Perth Western By-pass near Junction 11 of the M90.

STENHOUSEMUIR FC

Founded: 1884 (**Entered League**: 1921)
Former Names: Heather Rangers FC
Nickname: 'Warriors'
Ground: Ochilview Park, Gladstone Road, Stenhousemuir FK5 5QL
Ground Capacity: 2,654
Seating Capacity: 628

Record Attendance: 12,500 (11/3/50)
Pitch Size: 110 × 72 yards
Colours: Maroon shirts and shorts
Telephone Nº: (01324) 562992
Ticket Office: (01324) 562992
Fax Number: (01324) 562980
Web Site: www.stenhousemuirfc.com

GENERAL INFORMATION
Car Parking: A Large Car Park is adjacent
Coach Parking: Behind the North Terracing
Nearest Railway Station: Larbert (1 mile)
Nearest Bus Station: Falkirk (2½ miles)
Club Shop: At the ground
Opening Times: Weekdays from 9.00am to 5.00pm and also 4 hours before home games
Telephone Nº: (01324) 562992
Police Telephone Nº: (01324) 562112

GROUND INFORMATION
Away Supporters' Entrances & Sections: Terracing entrances and accommodation

ADMISSION INFO (2007/2008 PRICES)
Adult Standing: £9.00
Adult Seating: £10.00
Senior Citizen/Child Standing: £4.50
Senior Citizen/Child Seating: £5.00
Programme Price: £1.00

DISABLED INFORMATION
Wheelchairs: Accommodated
Helpers: Admitted
Prices: Normal prices are charged
Disabled Toilets: Available in the Gladstone Road Stand
Contact: (01324) 562992   (Bookings are not necessary)

Travelling Supporters' Information:
Routes: Exit the M876 at Junction 2 and follow signs for Stenhousemuir. Pass the Old Hospital and turn right after the Golf Course. The ground is on the left behind the houses – the floodlights are visible for ¼ mile.

STIRLING ALBION FC

Founded: 1945 (**Entered League**: 1946)
Nickname: 'The Albion'
Ground: Forthbank Stadium, Spring Kerse, Stirling, FK7 7UJ
Ground Capacity: 3,808
Seating Capacity: 2,508
Record Attendance: 3,808 (17/2/96)

Pitch Size: 110 × 74 yards
Colours: Shirts are Red with White trim, White Shorts
Telephone Nº: (01786) 450399
Ticket Office: (01786) 450399
Fax Number: (01786) 448400
Web site: None

GENERAL INFORMATION

Car Parking: Large Car Park ¾ mile from the ground
Coach Parking: Adjacent to the ground
Nearest Railway Station: Stirling (2 miles)
Nearest Bus Station: Stirling (2 miles)
Club Shop: At the ground
Opening Times: Weekdays and Matchdays 10.00am to 12.30pm and 2.30pm to 4.30pm
Telephone Nº: (01786) 450399
Police Telephone Nº: (01786) 456000

GROUND INFORMATION

Away Supporters' Entrances & Sections:
South Terracing and East Stand

ADMISSION INFO (2007/2008 PRICES)

Adult Standing: £13.00
Adult Seating: £14.00
Child Standing: £9.00
Child Seating: £10.00
Note: Standing admission is only available for certain games.
Family Section: Adult + 1 Child £22.00. Extra children are admitted at £8.00 each up to a maximum of 3 children
Programme Price: £2.00

DISABLED INFORMATION

Wheelchairs: 18 spaces each for home and away fans
Helpers: Admitted
Prices: Free of charge for the disabled and helpers
Disabled Toilets: 2 available beneath each stand
Contact: (01786) 450399 (Bookings are necessary)

Travelling Supporters' Information:
Routes: Follow signs for Stirling from the M9/M80 Northbound. From Pirnhall Roundabout follow signs for Alloa/St. Andrew's to the 4th roundabout and then turn left for the stadium.

STRANRAER FC

Founded: 1870 (**Entered League**: 1955)
Nickname: 'The Blues'
Ground: Stair Park, London Road, Stranraer, DG9 8BS
Ground Capacity: 5,600
Seating Capacity: 1,830
Record Attendance: 6,500 (24/1/48)

Pitch Size: 112 × 70 yards
Colours: Blue shirts with White shorts
Telephone Nº: (01776) 703271
Ticket Office: (01776) 703271
Fax Number: (01776) 889514
Web Site: www.stranraerfc.org

GENERAL INFORMATION
Car Parking: Car Park at the ground
Coach Parking: Port Rodie, Stranraer
Nearest Railway Station: Stranraer (1 mile)
Nearest Bus Station: Port Rodie, Stranraer
Club Shop: At the ground
Opening Times: 2.15pm to 3.00pm and during half-time on Matchdays only
Telephone Nº: None
Police Telephone Nº: (01776) 702112

GROUND INFORMATION
Away Supporters' Entrances & Sections:
London Road entrances for the Visitors Stand

ADMISSION INFO (2007/2008 PRICES)
Adult Standing: £10.00
Adult Seating: £12.00
Concessionary Standing: £5.00
Concessionary Seating: £6.00
Under-12s: Admitted free of charge with a paying adult
Programme Price: £1.00

DISABLED INFORMATION
Wheelchairs: 6 spaces each for Home and Away fans in front of the North Stand and South Stand
Helpers: Please phone the club for details
Prices: Please phone the club for details
Disabled Toilets: One in the North and South Stands
Contact: (01776) 889514 (Bookings are necessary)

Travelling Supporters' Information:
Routes: From the West: Take the A75 to Stranraer and the ground is on the left-hand side of the road in a public park shortly after entering the town; From the North: Take the A77 and follow it to where it joins with the A75 (then as West). The ground is set back from the road and the floodlights are clearly visible.

Also available from Soccer Books Ltd. –

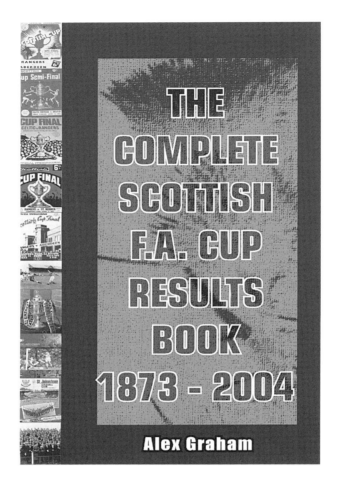

This statistical book lists the result of every match played in the Scottish F.A. Cup from 1873-2004.

Softback Price of each £ 19.95

Available from all good book shops or order direct –

Soccer Books Limited
72 St. Peters Avenue
Cleethorpes
DN35 8HU
United Kingdom

Web site– www.soccer-books.co.uk

THE HIGHLAND FOOTBALL LEAGUE

Founded   1893

Secretary   Mr J.H. Grant

Contact Address
35 Hamilton Drive, Elgin   IV30 2NN

Phone (01343) 544995

Web site   www.highlandfootballleague.com

Clubs for the 2007/2008 Season

BRORA RANGERS FC

Founded: 1878
Nickname: 'The Cattachs'
Ground: Dudgeon Park, Brora   KW9 6QA
Ground Capacity: 4,000
Seating Capacity: 250
Record Attendance: 2,000 (31/8/63)
Pitch Size: 112 × 70 yards

Colours: Shirts are Red with White underarm flashes, Shorts are Red
Telephone/Fax Nº: (01408) 621231
Social Club Phone Nº: (01408) 621570
Contact Phone Nº: (01408) 621114
Correspondence Address: Kevin Mackay, 2 Muirfield Road, Brora   KW9 6QP

GENERAL INFORMATION

Car Parking: Adjacent to the ground
Coach Parking: Adjacent to the ground
Nearest Railway Station: Brora
Nearest Bus Station: Brora
Club Shop: At the ground
Opening Times: Matchdays only
Telephone Nº: (01408) 621231
Police Telephone Nº: (01408) 621222

GROUND INFORMATION

Away Supporters' Entrances & Sections:
No usual segregation

ADMISSION INFO (2007/2008 PRICES)

Adult Standing: £6.00
Adult Seating: £7.00
Child Standing: £3.00
Child Seating: £4.00
Programme Price: £1.00

DISABLED INFORMATION

Wheelchairs: Accommodated
Helpers: Please phone the club for details
Prices: Please phone the club for details
Disabled Toilets: None at present (under construction)
Contact: (01408) 621231   (Bookings are necessary)

Travelling Supporters' Information:
Routes: Take the A9 Northbound from Inverness and the Stadium is situated on the right upon entering the town. It is clearly visible from the road.

BUCKIE THISTLE FC

Founded: 1889
Former Names: None
Nickname: 'The Jags'
Ground: Victoria Park, Midmar Street, Buckie, Banffshire
Ground Capacity: 5,000
Seating Capacity: 400
Record Attendance: 8,168 (1/3/58)

Pitch Size: 109 × 73 yards
Colours: Green and White hooped shirts, White shorts
Telephone Nº: (01542) 831454
Contact Address: Murray Duncan,
8 The Meadows, Buckie   AB56 1QG
Contact Nº: (01542) 835660
Web Site: www.buckiethistle.com

GENERAL INFORMATION

Car Parking: Adjacent to the ground
Coach Parking: Adjacent to the ground
Nearest Railway Station: Keith (12 miles)
Nearest Bus Station: Buckie
Club Shop: In the Supporters' Club inside the ground
Social Club: Victoria Park Function Hall at the ground
Social Club Telephone Nº: (01542) 831454
Police Telephone Nº: (01542) 832222

GROUND INFORMATION

Away Supporters' Entrances & Sections:
No usual segregation

ADMISSION INFO (2007/2008 PRICES)

Adult Standing: £6.00
Adult Seating: £7.00
Concessions Standing: £3.00
Concessions Seating: £4.00
Programme Price: £1.00

DISABLED INFORMATION

Wheelchairs: Accommodated in front of the stand
Helpers: Admitted
Prices: Normal prices apply
Disabled Toilets: Available in the Victoria Park Function Hall
Contact: (01542) 831454   (Bookings are helpful)

Travelling Supporters' Information:
Routes: From the East and West: Exit the A98 onto the A942 towards Buckie. Go straight on at the roundabout and travel along Buckie High Street. Turn left at the roundabout next to Cluny Square into West Church Street then take the 1st left into South Pringle Street. The ground is straight ahead.

CLACHNACUDDIN FC

Founded: 1886
Nickname: 'Lilywhites'
Ground: Grant Street Park, Wyvis Place, Inverness, IV3 6DR
Ground Capacity: 2,500
Seating Capacity: 154
Record Attendance: 9,000 (27/8/51)
Pitch Size: 108 × 70 yards

Colours: White shirts with Black shorts
Telephone Nº: (01463) 238825
Ticket Information: (01463) 718261
Fax Number: (01463) 718261
Contact Address: Gilbert Skinner, 1 Duncraig Court, Duncraig Street, Inverness   IV3 5DE
Contact Phone Nº: (07810) 540398
E-mail: clachnacuddinfc@highlandleague.com

GENERAL INFORMATION

Car Parking: Adjacent to the ground
Coach Parking: Adjacent to the ground
Nearest Railway Station: Inverness
Nearest Bus Station: Inverness
Club Shop: At the ground
Opening Times: Matchdays only
Telephone Nº: (01463) 238825
Police Telephone Nº: (01463) 715555

GROUND INFORMATION

Away Supporters' Entrances & Sections:
No usual segregation

ADMISSION INFO (2007/2008 PRICES)

Adult Standing: £6.00
Adult Seating: £7.00
Child Standing: £3.00
Child Seating: £4.00
Programme Price: £1.00

DISABLED INFORMATION

Wheelchairs: Accommodated
Helpers: Admitted
Prices: Normal prices apply
Disabled Toilets: Available
Contact: (01463) 238825   (Bookings are not necessary)

Travelling Supporters' Information:
Routes: From the East and South: From the roundabout at the junction of the A9 and A96, proceed into the Town Centre and over the River Ness. Turn right at the traffic lights (onto the A862 to Dingwall), go up Kenneth Street and over the roundabout onto Telford Street for 200 yards before turning right into Telford Road opposite the Fish Shop. At the top, turn left onto Lower Kessack Street and left again. Finally, turn left into Wyvis Place and the ground is on the left.

COVE RANGERS FC

Founded: 1922
Nickname: None
Ground: Allan Park, Loirston Road, Cove, Aberdeen, AB12 4NS
Ground Capacity: 2,300
Seating Capacity: 100
Record Attendance: 2,300 (15/11/92)
Pitch Size: 104× 65 yards

Colours: Blue shirts and shorts
Telephone Nº: (01224) 871467 (Social Club)
Fax Number: (01224) 895199
Contact Address: Duncan Little, c/o Club
Contact Phone Nº: (01224) 890433 (Matchdays) or (01224) 896282 (Evenings)
Social Club Nº: (01224) 871467
Web Site: www.eteamz.com/coverangers

GENERAL INFORMATION

Car Parking: School Car Park/Loirston Road
Coach Parking: By Police direction
Nearest Railway Station: Guild Street, Aberdeen
Nearest Bus Station: Guild Street, Aberdeen
Club Shop: At the Social Club
Opening Times: Matchdays Only
Telephone Nº: (01224) 871467
Police Telephone Nº: (01224) 639111

GROUND INFORMATION

Away Supporters' Entrances & Sections:
Loirston Road entrances and accommodation

ADMISSION INFO (2007/2008 PRICES)

Adult Standing: £6.00
Adult Seating: £6.00
Child Standing: £3.00
Child Seating: £3.00
Programme Price: £1.00

DISABLED INFORMATION

Wheelchairs: Accommodated
Helpers: Admitted
Prices: Free of charge for the disabled
Disabled Toilets: Available in the Social Club
Are Bookings Necessary: No, but preferable
Contact: (01224) 890433 (Duncan Little) (Matchdays); (01224) 896282 (Evenings)

Travelling Supporters' Information:
Routes: From the North: Follow signs to Altens and Cove and take the Cove turn-off at the Altens Thistle Hotel roundabout along Loirston Road – the ground is ½ mile on the right; From the South: Take the Aberdeen Harbour turn-off some 10 miles north of Stonehaven and continue to Altens Thistle Hotel roundabout – then as from the North.
Bus Routes: No.13 bus runs from the City Centre to the ground.

DEVERONVALE FC

Founded: 1938
Nickname: 'The Vale'
Ground: Princess Royal Park, Airlie Gardens, Banff, AB45 1AZ
Ground Capacity: 2,651
Seating Capacity: 418
Record Attendance: 5,000 (27/4/52)
Pitch Size: 109 × 78 yards

Colours: Shirts are Red with White trim, White shorts
Telephone Nº: (01261) 818303
Fax Number: (01261) 813753
Contact Address: Stewart McPherson, 8 Victoria Place, Banff AB45 1EL
Contact Phone Nº: (01261) 818303
Web Site: www.deveronvale.co.uk
E-mail: deveronvalefc@highlandleague.com

GENERAL INFORMATION

Car Parking: Street parking
Coach Parking: Bridge Road Car Park
Nearest Railway Station: Keith (20 miles)
Nearest Bus Station: Macduff (1 mile)
Club Shop: At the ground
Opening Times: Matchdays only
Telephone Nº: (01261) 818303
Police Telephone Nº: 0845 600-5700

GROUND INFORMATION

Away Supporters' Entrances & Sections:
No usual segregation

ADMISSION INFO (2007/2008 PRICES)

Adult Standing: £6.00
Adult Seating: £7.00
Child Standing: £3.00
Child Seating: £4.00
Programme Price: £1.50

DISABLED INFORMATION

Wheelchairs: Accommodated
Helpers: Admitted
Prices: Please phone the club for details
Disabled Toilets: Available
Contact: (01261) 818303 (Bookings are necessary)

Travelling Supporters' Information:
Routes: From Aberdeen: Enter the town at Banff Bridge – the ground is situated ¼ mile along on the right; From Inverness: Travel through Banff on the main bypass and the ground is situated on the left, ¼ mile before Banff Bridge.

FORRES MECHANICS FC

Founded: 1884
Nickname: 'Can Cans'
Ground: Mosset Park, Lea Road, Forres IV36 0AU
Ground Capacity: 6,540
Seating Capacity: 540
Record Attendance: 7,000 (2/2/57)
Pitch Size: 106 × 69 yards

Colours: Maroon & Gold striped shirts, Maroon shorts
Telephone/Fax Number: (01309) 675096
Contact Address: David W. Macdonald, Secretary, 7 Brinuth Place, Elgin IV30 6YW
Contact Phone N°: (01343) 544294
Mobile Phone Contact N°: 07779 782799
Web site: None

GENERAL INFORMATION

Car Parking: At the ground
Coach Parking: At the ground
Nearest Railway Station: Forres
Nearest Bus Station: Forres
Club Shop: At the ground
Opening Times: Matchdays only
Telephone N°: (01309) 675096
Police Telephone N°: (01309) 672224

GROUND INFORMATION

Away Supporters' Entrances & Sections:
No usual segregation

ADMISSION INFO (2007/2008 PRICES)

Adult Standing: £6.00
Adult Seating: £7.00
Child/Senior Citizen Standing: £3.00
Child/Senior Citizen Seating: £4.00
Programme Price: £1.00

DISABLED INFORMATION

Wheelchairs: Accommodated
Helpers: Admitted
Prices: Normal prices apply
Disabled Toilets: One available
Contact: (01309) 675096   (Bookings are not necessary)

Travelling Supporters' Information:
Routes: From A96 East (Inverness): Turn off the A96 onto the B9011. Continue along this road and pass Tesco, turn left at the roundabout then immediately right into Invererne Road. Follow for about ½ mile then turn right across Lea Bridge then left for the ground; From A96 West (Aberdeen): Drive into Forres on the A96 passing the ground on your left. After a short distance, turn left onto the A940 (Market Street). Immediately before the roundabout turn left into Invererne Road. Then as above.

FORT WILLIAM FC

Founded: 1984
Nickname: 'The Fort'
Ground: Claggan Park, Fort William, Inverness-shire
Ground Capacity: 4,000
Seating Capacity: 400
Record Attendance: 1,500 (4/1/86)
Pitch Size: 102 × 80 yards

Colours: Gold and Black shirts with Black shorts
Telephone Nº: None at the ground
Contact Address: James Campbell,
54 Drumfada Terrace, Corpach, Fort William PH33 7LA
Contact Phone Nº: (01397) 772298
Contact Fax Number: (01397) 772298

GENERAL INFORMATION

Car Parking: At the ground
Coach Parking: At the ground
Nearest Railway Station: Fort William
Nearest Bus Station: Fort William
Club Shop: None
Police Telephone Nº: (01397) 702361

GROUND INFORMATION

Away Supporters' Entrances & Sections:
No usual segregation

ADMISSION INFO (2007/2008 PRICES)

Adult Standing: £6.00
Adult Seating: £6.00
Child Standing: £3.00 (under 12's are admitted free
Child Seating: £3.00   with a paying adult)
Programme Price: £1.00

DISABLED INFORMATION

Wheelchairs: Accommodated
Helpers: Please phone the club for details
Prices: Please phone the club for details
Disabled Toilets: None
Contact: (01397) 772298   (Bookings are not necessary)

Travelling Supporters' Information:
Routes: From the South: Approaching Fort William on the A82, proceed on the bypass of the Town Centre. After 2 roundabouts continue on Belford Road past the Railway Station on the left and the Swimming Baths on the right. After ½ mile and crossing over the River Nevis, take the first right into Claggan Road and the ground is ½ mile on the left; From Inverness: Take the A98 into Fort William before taking the 2nd left after the Shell petrol into Claggan Road. Take the 1st right before Spar signposted for the Ben Nevis Footpath. The ground is 1st left opposite the footbridge.

FRASERBURGH FC

Founded: 1910
Nickname: 'The Broch'
Ground: Bellslea Park, Seaforth Street, Fraserburgh, AB43 9BD
Ground Capacity: 3,000
Seating Capacity: 480
Record Attendance: 5,800 (13/2/54)
Pitch Size: 106 × 66 yards

Colours: Black and White striped shirts, Black shorts
Telephone Nº: (01346) 518444
Contact Address: Finlay Noble, 18 Bawdley Head, Fraserburgh AB43 9SE
Contact Phone Nº: (01346) 513474
Mobile Phone Contact Nº: 0774 700-3806
Web Site: www.fraserburghfc.net

GENERAL INFORMATION
Car Parking: At the ground
Coach Parking: At the ground
Nearest Railway Station: Aberdeen (40 miles)
Nearest Bus Station: Fraserburgh
Club Shop: Duthie & Bruce, 5 Saltoun Square, Fraserburgh
Opening Times: Monday to Saturday 9.00am to 5.00pm
Telephone Nº: (01346) 518769
Police Telephone Nº: (01346) 513121

GROUND INFORMATION
Away Supporters' Entrances & Sections:
No usual segregation

ADMISSION INFO (2007/2008 PRICES)
Adult Standing: £6.00
Adult Seating: £7.00
Child Standing: £3.00
Child Seating: £4.00
Programme Price: £1.00

DISABLED INFORMATION
Wheelchairs: Accommodated
Helpers: Admitted
Prices: Normal prices apply
Disabled Toilets: Available
Contact: (01346) 518444 (Bookings are not necessary)

Travelling Supporters' Information:
Routes: The ground is situated in the Town Centre, off Seaforth Street.

HUNTLY FC

Founded: 1928
Nickname: None
Ground: Christie Park, East Park Street, Huntly, Aberdeenshire AB54 8JE
Ground Capacity: 4,500
Seating Capacity: 270
Record Attendance: 4,500 (18/2/95)
Pitch Size: 105 × 72 yards

Colours: Black and Gold shirts with Black shorts
Telephone Nº: (01466) 793548
Social Club Phone Nº: (01466) 793680
Contact Address: Brien Ross, c/o R & M Engineering, Steven Road, Huntly AB54 8SX
Contact Phone Nº: (01466) 793286
Web Site: www.huntlyfc.co.uk

GENERAL INFORMATION

Car Parking: At the ground
Coach Parking: At the ground
Nearest Railway Station: Huntly (1 mile)
Nearest Bus Station: Huntly (¼ mile)
Club Shop: At the ground
Opening Times: Matchdays only
Police Telephone Nº: (01466) 792246

GROUND INFORMATION

Away Supporters' Entrances & Sections:
No usual segregation

ADMISSION INFO (2007/2008 PRICES)

Adult Standing: £6.00
Adult Seating: £7.00
Child Standing: £3.00
Child Seating: £4.00
Programme Price: £1.00

DISABLED INFORMATION

Wheelchairs: Accommodated
Helpers: Please phone the club for details
Prices: Please phone the club for details
Disabled Toilets: None
Contact: (01466) 793269 (Bookings are not necessary)

Travelling Supporters' Information:
Routes: Enter Town off the A96 and proceed along King George V Avenue and Gordon Street. Pass through the Town Centre Square, along Castle Street to East Park Street and the ground is on the right before the Castle.

INVERURIE LOCO WORKS FC

Founded: 1903
Nickname: 'Locos'
Ground: Harlaw Park, Harlaw Road, Inverurie, Aberdeenshire
Ground Capacity: 2,500
Seating Capacity: 250
Record Attendance: 2,150
Pitch Size: 110 × 70 yards

Colours: Red and Black striped shirts, Black shorts
Telephone Nº: (01467) 623055
Fax Number: (01467) 622168
Contact Address: Gordon Park, 13 Golf Crescent, Inverurie AB51 3QU
Contact Phone Nº: (01467) 621347
Web Site: www.inverurielocoworks.com

GENERAL INFORMATION
Car Parking: At the ground
Coach Parking: At the ground
Nearest Railway Station: Inverurie
Nearest Bus Station: –
Club Shop: Limited supply of merchandise available

GROUND INFORMATION
Away Supporters' Entrances & Sections:
No usual segregation

ADMISSION INFO (2007/2008 PRICES)
Adult Standing: £7.00
Adult Seating: £7.00
Child/Senior Citizen Standing: £4.00
Child/Senior Citizen Seating: £4.00
Programme Price: £1.00

DISABLED INFORMATION
Wheelchairs: Accommodated in the Covered Enclosure
Helpers: Admitted
Prices: Normal prices apply
Disabled Toilets: Available
Contact: (01467) 621347 or 07816 604434

Travelling Supporters' Information:
Routes: From the North: Take the A96 to the Inverurie bypass then turn left at the Safeways roundabout along Blackhall Road and left at the next roundabout into Boroughmuir Drive. Cross the next roundabout and then turn 1st right into Hawlaw Road for the ground; From the South: Take the A96 to the Inverurie bypass then as above.

KEITH FC

Founded: 1910
Nickname: 'Maroons'
Ground: Kynoch Park, Balloch Road, Keith AB55 5EN
Ground Capacity: 4,500
Seating Capacity: 450
Record Attendance: 5,820 (4/2/28)
Pitch Size: 110 × 75 yards

Colours: Shirts and shorts are Maroon with Blue trim
Telephone N°: (01542) 882629
Fax Number: (01542) 882631
Contact Phone N°: (01542) 882629
Mobile Phone Contact N°: 07814 431760
Web Site: www.keith-fc.co.uk
E-mail: keithfc@highlandleague.com

GENERAL INFORMATION

Car Parking: Street parking in Balloch Road, Moss Street and Reidhaven Square
Coach Parking: Balloch Road or Bridge Street Coach Park
Nearest Railway Station: Keith (1 mile)
Nearest Bus Station: Keith
Club Shop: At the ground
Opening Times: Wednesday to Friday 9.00am to 12.30pm
Telephone N°: (01542) 882629
Police Telephone N°: (01542) 882502

GROUND INFORMATION

Away Supporters' Entrances & Sections:
No usual segregation except for some Cup Ties

ADMISSION INFO (2007/2008 PRICES)

Adult Standing: £6.00
Adult Seating: £7.00
Child Standing: £3.00
Child Seating: £4.00
Programme Price: £1.00

DISABLED INFORMATION

Wheelchairs: Accommodated
Helpers: Admitted
Prices: Normal prices apply
Disabled Toilets: None

Travelling Supporters' Information:
Routes: From Inverness: Follow the A96 through Keith before turning left opposite the newsagents and public toilets in Reidhaven Square. Follow signs for the Moray College Learning Centre, take the next left into Balloch Road and the ground is on the right; From Aberdeen: After Entering Keith turn right opposite the newsagents in Reidhaven Square. Then as above.

LOSSIEMOUTH FC

Founded: 1945
Nickname: 'Coasters'
Ground: Grant Park, Kellas Avenue, Lossiemouth
IV31 6JG
Ground Capacity: 3,500
Seating Capacity: 250
Record Attendance: 2,700 (28/12/48)
Pitch Size: 110 × 67 yards

Colours: Red shirts and shorts
Telephone Nº: (01343) 813717
Fax Number: (01343) 815440
Social Club Nº: (01343) 813168
Contact Address: Alan McIntosh, 3 Forties Place,
Lossiemouth IV31 6SS
Contact Phone Nº: (01343) 813328 & (07890) 749053
Contact e-mail: alanlfcsec@aol.com

GENERAL INFORMATION

Car Parking: At the ground
Coach Parking: At the ground
Nearest Railway Station: Elgin
Nearest Bus Station: Lossiemouth
Club Shop: At the ground
Opening Times: Matchdays only
Telephone Nº: (01343) 813168
Police Telephone Nº: (01343) 812022

GROUND INFORMATION

Away Supporters' Entrances & Sections:
No usual segregation

ADMISSION INFO (2007/2008 PRICES)

Adult Standing: £6.00
Adult Seating: £6.00
Child Standing: £3.00 (Free when accompanied by adult)
Child Seating: £3.00
Programme Price: £1.00

DISABLED INFORMATION

Wheelchairs: Accommodated
Helpers: Admitted
Prices: Free of charge for the disabled
Disabled Toilets: Available
Contact: (01343) 813328 (Alan McIntosh) (Please book)

Travelling Supporters' Information:
Routes: Take the A941 to Lossiemouth. As you enter the town take the 3rd turning on the right into Moray Street. Continue along Moray Street then take the 4th turning on the right into Kellas Avenue. Grant Park is at the end of this road.

NAIRN COUNTY FC

Founded: 1914
Nickname: 'The Wee County'
Ground: Station Park, Balblair Road, Nairn IV12 5LT
Ground Capacity: 3,800
Seating Capacity: 250
Record Attendance: 4,000 (2/9/50)
Pitch Size: 110 × 62 yards

Colours: Maize Yellow shirts with Black border, Black shorts
Telephone Nº: (01667) 454298
Fax Number: (01667) 462510
Contact Address: John McNeill, 50 Station Road, Ardersier, Inverness IV2 7ST
Contact Phone Nº: (01667) 462510
Web Site: www.nairncountyfc.com

GENERAL INFORMATION

Car Parking: At the ground
Coach Parking: At the ground
Nearest Railway Station: Nairn (adjacent)
Nearest Bus Station: King Street, Nairn (½ mile)
Club Shop: At the Social Club
Opening Times: Club hours only
Telephone Nº: (01667) 453286
Police Telephone Nº: (01667) 452222

GROUND INFORMATION

Away Supporters' Entrances & Sections:
No usual segregation

ADMISSION INFO (2007/2008 PRICES)

Adult Standing: £6.00
Adult Seating: £7.00
Senior Citizen/Child Standing: £3.00
Senior Citizen/Child Seating: £4.00
Programme Price: £1.00

DISABLED INFORMATION

Wheelchairs: Accommodated in the Stand
Helpers: Admitted
Prices: £4.00 for the disabled
Disabled Toilets: None
Contact: (01667) 462510 (Bookings are not necessary)

Travelling Supporters' Information:
Routes: The ground is situated on the south side of Nairn at the bottom of the Main Street, adjacent to the Railway Station.

ROTHES FC

Founded: 1938
Former Names: Rothes Victoria FC
Nickname: 'The Speysiders'
Ground: Mackessack Park, Rothes   AB38 7BY
Ground Capacity: 2,650
Seating Capacity: 160
Record Attendance: 2,054 (September 1946)
Pitch Size: 108 × 74 yards

Colours: Tangerine shirts with Black shorts
Telephone N°: (01340) 831972
Social Club N°: (01340) 831348
Fax Number: None
Contact Address: Brian Cameron, 35 Land Street, Rothes, Aberlour   AB38 7BA
Contact Phone N°: (01340) 832387
Web Site: None

GENERAL INFORMATION

Car Parking: At the ground
Coach Parking: At the ground
Nearest Railway Station: Elgin
Nearest Bus Station: Elgin
Club Shop: None
Nearest Police Station: Rothes
Police Telephone N°: (01340) 831341

GROUND INFORMATION

Away Supporters' Entrances & Sections:
No usual segregation

ADMISSION INFO (2007/2008 PRICES)

Adult Standing: £6.00
Adult Seating: £7.00
Child Standing: £3.00
Child Seating: £3.50
Programme Price: £1.00

DISABLED INFORMATION

Wheelchairs: Accommodated
Helpers: Admitted
Prices: Normal prices apply
Disabled Toilets: Available
Contact: (01340) 831344 (Bookings are not necessary)

Travelling Supporters' Information:
Routes: From the A96 take the A941 signposted for Perth and follow into Rothes. After entering the town take the 2nd exit (A941 Perth) before immediately turning 1st left down a small track. Follow this past the distillery to reach the ground.

WICK ACADEMY FC

Founded: 1893
Nickname: 'The Scorries'
Ground: Harmsworth Park, South Road, Wick, Caithness KW1 5NH
Ground Capacity: 2,000
Seating Capacity: 133
Record Attendance: 2,000 (30/7/84)
Pitch Size: 106 × 76 yards

Colours: Black and White striped shirts, White shorts
Telephone Nº: (01955) 602446
Fax Number: (01955) 602446
Contact Address: Mr A. Ross, 29 East Banks, Wick, Caithness KW1 5NL
Contact Phone Nº: (01955) 603883
(Mobile 07790 728823)
Web Site: www.wick-academy.co.uk

GENERAL INFORMATION

Car Parking: At the ground
Coach Parking: At the ground
Nearest Railway Station: Wick (10 minutes walk)
Nearest Bus Station: Wick
Club Shop: Wick Sports Shop, High Street, Wick
Opening Times: 9.00am to 5.00pm
Telephone Nº: (01955) 602930
Police Telephone Nº: (01955) 603551

GROUND INFORMATION

Away Supporters' Entrances & Sections:
No usual segregation

ADMISSION INFO (2007/2008 PRICES)

Adult Standing: £6.00
Adult Seating: £6.00
Child Stand ng: £3.00
Child Seating: £3.00
Programme Price: £1.00

DISABLED INFORMATION

Wheelchairs: 2 spaces available in the North Stand
Helpers: Please phone the club for details
Prices: Please phone the club for details
Disabled Toilets: None
Contact: (01955) 603883 (Bookings are not necessary)

Travelling Supporters' Information:
Routes: The ground is situated on the A99 road from Inverness beside the Cemetery.

STATISTICS
SEASONS 2004/2005, 2005/2006 & 2006/2007

Scottish Premier League
Home & Away Chart • Final League Table

Scottish Football League Division One
Home & Away Chart • Final League Table

Scottish Football League Division Two
Home & Away Chart • Final League Table

Scottish Football League Division Three
Home & Away Chart • Final League Table

STATISTICS
SEASON 2006/2007

Highland Football League
Home & Away Chart • Final League Table

Scottish Cup • Scottish League Cup

Scottish League Challenge Cup

2004-2005 Scottish Premier League	Aberdeen	Celtic	Dundee	Dundee United	Dunfermline Athletic	Heart of Midlothian	Hibernian	Inverness CT	Kilmarnock	Livingstone	Motherwell	Rangers
Aberdeen FC		0-2	1-1	---	---	2-0	3-0	---	---	2-0	1-3	1-2
		0-1	1-1	1-0	2-1	0-1	0-1	0-0	3-2	2-0	2-1	0-0
Celtic FC	3-2		---	3-0	6-0	0-2	1-3	---	---	---	2-0	---
	2-3		3-0	1-0	3-0	3-0	2-1	3-0	2-1	2-1	2-0	1-0
Dundee FC	---	---		1-2	2-1	1-1	---	1-1	1-0	0-1	---	0-2
	1-0	2-2		1-0	1-2	0-1	1-4	3-1	3-1	0-0	1-2	0-2
Dundee United FC	1-2	2-3	2-2		0-1	2-1	---	1-1	1-1	1-1	---	---
	1-1	0-3	1-2		1-2	1-1	1-4	2-1	3-0	1-0	0-1	1-1
Dunfermline Athletic FC	---	---	5-0	1-1		1-1	1-4	0-0	0-4	0-2	0-0	0-1
	0-1	0-2	3-1	1-1		1-0	1-1	1-1	4-1	0-0	1-1	1-2
Heart of Midlothian FC	1-0	1-2	---	---	---		1-2	0-2	---	3-1	0-0	1-2
	0-0	0-2	3-0	3-2	3-0		2-1	1-0	3-0	0-0	0-1	0-0
Hibernian FC	1-2	1-3	4-0	3-2	---	2-2		---	3-0	0-3	---	0-1
	2-1	2-2	4-4	2-0	2-1	1-1		2-1	0-1	2-1	1-0	0-1
Inverness Caledonian Thistle FC	0-1	0-2	3-2	0-1	2-0	---	3-0		1-2	0-1	1-0	---
	1-3	1-3	2-1	1-1	2-0	1-1	1-2		0-2	2-0	1-1	1-1
Kilmarnock FC	0-1	0-1	1-0	3-0	2-1	---	---	0-1		2-0	---	---
	0-1	2-4	3-1	5-2	1-0	1-1	3-1	2-2		1-3	2-0	0-1
Livingston FC	---	0-4	1-1	---	1-1	---	---	1-4	3-1		1-1	---
	0-2	2-4	1-0	1-1	2-0	1-2	0-2	3-0	0-2		2-3	1-4
Motherwell FC	0-1	2-1	---	2-0	---	2-0	2-2	---	1-1	---		2-3
	0-0	2-3	3-0	4-2	2-1	2-0	1-2	1-2	0-1	2-0		0-2
Rangers FC	3-1	1-2	---	0-1	---	2-1	---	1-1	2-1	3-0	4-1	
	5-0	2-0	3-0	1-1	3-0	3-2	4-1	1-0	2-0	4-0	4-1	

Scottish Premier League

Season 2004/2005

Rangers	38	29	6	3	78	22	93
Celtic	38	30	2	6	85	35	92
Hibernian	38	18	7	13	64	57	61
Aberdeen	38	18	7	13	44	39	61
Heart of Midlothian	38	13	11	14	43	41	50
Motherwell	38	13	9	16	46	49	48
Kilmarnock	38	15	4	19	49	55	49
Inverness Caledonian Thistle	38	11	11	16	41	47	44
Dundee United	38	8	12	18	41	59	36
Livingston	38	9	8	21	34	61	35
Dunfermline Athletic	38	8	10	20	34	60	34
Dundee	38	8	9	21	37	71	33

With 5 games of the season left, the Division was split into two groups of 6. The top half contended for the Championship while the bottom half decided relegation.

2004-2005 Scottish Football League Division 1	Airdrie United	Clyde	Falkirk	Hamilton Academical	Partick Thistle	Queen of the South	Raith Rovers	Ross County	St. Johnstone	St. Mirren
Airdrie United FC		2-4	2-2	1-0	0-1	2-0	2-1	2-1	0-0	0-2
		3-1	1-3	0-2	4-2	0-1	1-1	1-2	1-0	3-2
Clyde FC	1-0		0-1	1-3	1-1	0-1	1-0	1-0	1-1	0-0
	1-2		0-2	2-1	2-1	2-0	2-0	1-0	1-0	0-0
Falkirk FC	1-0	0-0		1-1	2-1	1-2	2-0	1-0	3-0	1-2
	5-0	1-1		1-1	3-0	4-2	4-2	2-2	3-1	0-0
Hamilton Academical FC	1-1	0-1	1-0		1-0	1-1	1-0	0-1	0-3	0-0
	1-3	0-1	0-1		0-1	1-0	2-0	1-2	1-1	2-2
Partick Thistle FC	1-1	1-0	2-1	1-1		3-1	4-1	0-0	0-4	0-0
	3-2	0-0	1-4	0-1		1-2	2-0	4-0	0-4	0-3
Queen of the South FC	0-0	0-1	1-1	1-2	3-1		1-1	1-0	2-0	0-0
	1-0	0-1	1-3	1-1	1-0		2-0	0-1	0-1	2-1
Raith Rovers FC	0-1	3-3	3-3	0-2	2-1	0-1		1-4	1-2	2-0
	0-2	2-3	0-2	2-2	0-0	1-2		1-2	1-0	0-3
Ross County FC	3-1	1-1	0-1	2-1	2-1	1-1	2-0		4-0	0-1
	1-2	0-1	0-1	1-1	0-1	1-0	1-1		0-1	1-1
St. Johnstone FC	1-2	0-0	0-3	0-2	1-1	0-0	2-0	0-2		0-0
	1-1	3-0	1-2	3-0	2-1	1-3	1-0	1-1		1-0
St. Mirren FC	1-0	0-0	0-1	0-1	1-1	3-0	3-0	1-0	1-1	
	1-1	0-0	2-0	1-0	2-1	2-2	1-0	3-2	2-1	

Scottish League Division One

Season 2004/2005

Falkirk	36	22	9	5	66	30	75
St. Mirren	36	15	15	6	41	23	60
Clyde	36	16	12	8	35	29	60
Queen of the South	36	14	9	13	36	38	51
Airdrie United	36	14	8	14	44	48	50
Ross County	36	13	8	15	40	37	47
Hamilton Academical	36	12	11	13	35	36	47
St. Johnstone	36	12	10	14	38	39	46
Partick Thistle	36	10	9	17	38	52	39
Raith Rovers	36	3	7	26	26	67	16

2004-2005 Scottish Football League Division 2	Alloa Athletic	Arbroath	Ayr United	Berwick Rangers	Brechin City	Dumbarton	Forfar Athletic	Greenock Morton	Stirling Albion	Stranraer
Alloa Athletic FC		2-2	5-1	2-2	1-1	4-2	0-2	2-2	3-0	3-0
		4-2	1-3	2-2	2-2	3-2	2-3	1-6	1-1	1-2
Arbroath FC	2-1		2-0	2-0	1-4	2-1	1-2	0-1	3-2	0-4
	0-3		0-0	1-1	2-2	0-2	0-2	0-3	2-1	0-1
Ayr United FC	1-1	2-2		0-1	0-1	1-1	1-0	2-1	0-3	0-0
	4-3	1-1		2-1	0-1	0-1	3-3	2-0	3-2	0-1
Berwick Rangers FC	2-1	2-3	2-1		2-1	0-3	1-1	2-2	2-2	1-2
	2-3	0-3	0-1		0-2	0-4	1-0	2-1	0-1	1-2
Brechin City FC	2-3	4-3	3-0	1-1		0-2	0-3	1-2	5-3	2-1
	4-0	4-1	5-0	4-1		4-0	2-0	2-1	0-3	4-1
Dumbarton FC	3-2	3-0	1-1	1-1	1-1		1-1	3-0	0-2	1-1
	0-1	1-3	1-0	3-1	1-1		0-1	0-3	1-1	1-3
Forfar Athletic FC	1-1	1-1	1-0	0-2	1-3	6-0		0-0	4-1	1-2
	3-1	5-0	2-3	1-1	1-0	0-2		2-0	0-2	0-1
Greenock Morton FC	2-0	2-0	2-1	4-2	0-2	0-0	4-0		2-0	2-0
	2-2	2-1	0-1	2-0	0-3	3-0	2-1		3-0	3-1
Stirling Albion FC	0-4	0-3	2-0	0-1	1-2	3-0	3-2	1-1		1-1
	2-0	5-2	1-1	3-1	1-5	1-0	3-1	1-1		1-1
Stranraer FC	0-1	3-3	1-3	1-0	0-1	2-1	0-0	1-1	0-3	
	3-0	2-1	2-1	2-2	4-2	1-0	1-0	1-0	0-0	

Scottish League Division Two

Season 2004/2005

Brechin City	36	22	6	8	81	43	72
Stranraer	36	18	9	9	48	41	63
Greenock Morton	36	18	8	10	60	37	62
Stirling Albion	36	14	9	13	56	55	51
Forfar Athletic	36	13	8	15	51	45	47
Alloa Athletic	36	12	10	14	66	68	46
Dumbarton	36	11	9	16	43	53	42
Ayr United	36	11	9	16	39	54	42
Arbroath	36	10	8	18	49	73	38
Berwick Rangers	36	8	10	18	40	64	34

2004-2005 Scottish Football League Division 3	Albion Rovers	Cowdenbeath	East Fife	East Stirlingshire	Elgin City	Gretna	Montrose	Peterhead	Queen's Park	Stenhousemuir
Albion Rovers FC		1-4	0-6	1-1	2-0	0-5	1-2	0-4	1-2	1-1
		2-3	2-0	3-3	2-2	2-6	1-2	0-1	0-4	1-0
Cowdenbeath FC	1-2		4-2	3-2	1-1	0-1	0-0	4-0	1-0	0-2
	2-0		1-1	2-1	3-1	0-8	0-0	0-4	2-1	0-6
East Fife FC	1-1	1-1		2-0	1-2	0-2	1-0	1-2	0-1	2-0
	1-0	1-1		1-0	2-0	1-3	1-0	0-2	1-4	0-0
East Stirlingshire FC	0-2	2-1	1-0		0-3	0-4	1-2	1-5	3-1	1-4
	1-1	0-2	1-1		0-1	1-2	1-1	1-2	0-5	3-2
Elgin City FC	1-1	2-0	2-1	0-0		2-6	2-2	0-2	1-0	4-2
	1-0	0-4	2-1	1-3		1-3	1-3	2-2	1-0	1-1
Gretna FC	6-2	2-0	4-0	1-0	2-1		4-1	6-1	4-0	7-0
	6-0	2-1	5-1	8-1	3-0		1-0	2-1	4-1	3-0
Montrose FC	0-1	1-2	2-2	4-1	2-0	0-4		0-2	2-0	0-3
	1-1	3-1	2-1	4-1	2-0	2-3		0-1	2-4	0-2
Peterhead FC	2-3	1-1	0-0	3-0	3-0	4-2	4-1		1-1	1-1
	4-1	3-1	2-0	5-0	2-1	1-1	3-2		2-2	5-0
Queen's Park FC	0-3	2-3	2-1	2-0	1-0	1-1	1-0	1-1		0-0
	1-1	3-2	1-2	0-0	0-1	3-2	1-2	1-2		4-3
Stenhousemuir FC	1-1	1-1	1-2	3-2	4-0	1-4	0-1	1-1	0-0	
	3-0	2-2	5-2	6-0	0-2	0-3	1-1	1-2	1-1	

Scottish League Division Three

Season 2004/2005

Gretna	36	32	2	2	130	29	98
Peterhead	36	23	9	4	81	38	78
Cowdenbeath	36	14	9	13	54	61	51
Queen's Park	36	13	9	14	51	50	48
Montrose	36	13	7	16	47	53	46
Elgin City	36	12	7	17	39	61	43
Stenhousemuir	36	10	12	14	58	58	42
East Fife	36	10	8	18	40	56	38
Albion Rovers	36	8	10	18	40	78	34
East Stirlingshire	36	5	7	24	32	88	22

Scottish Premier League 2005/2006	Aberdeen	Celtic	Dundee United	Dunfermline	Falkirk	Heart of Midlothian	Hibernian	Inverness Cal. Thistle	Kilmarnock	Livingston	Motherwell	Rangers
Aberdeen FC		2-2	---	---	1-0	0-1	1-0	---	2-2	3-0	2-2	2-0
		1-3	2-0	0-0	3-0	1-1	0-1	0-0	1-2	0-0	2-2	3-2
Celtic FC	3-0		3-3	---	2-1	1-0	1-1	2-1	2-0	---	---	0-0
	2-0		2-0	0-1	3-1	1-1	3-2	2-1	4-2	2-1	5-0	3-0
Dundee United FC	1-1	---		0-1	0-2	1-1	---	2-4	2-2	3-1	1-1	1-4
	1-1	2-4		2-1	2-1	0-3	1-0	1-1	0-0	2-0	1-1	0-0
Dunfermline Athletic FC	1-0	1-8	1-1		1-1	---	---	2-2	---	3-2	1-1	---
	0-2	0-4	2-1		0-1	1-4	1-2	0-1	0-1	0-1	0-3	3-3
Falkirk FC	---	---	1-0	0-0		1-2	0-0	1-4	---	1-0	1-1	1-2
	1-2	0-3	1-3	1-2		2-2	0-2	0-2	1-2	1-1	0-1	1-1
Heart of Midlothian FC	1-2	3-0	---	4-0	---		4-1	---	2-0	---	3-0	1-1
	2-0	2-3	3-0	2-0	5-0		4-0	0-0	1-0	2-1	2-1	1-0
Hibernian FC	0-4	1-2	3-1	3-1	---	2-1		0-2	2-1	7-0	---	1-2
	1-2	0-1	2-1	1-1	2-3	2-0		1-2	4-2	3-0	2-1	2-1
Inverness Caledonian Thistle	0-1	---	1-0	1-0	2-0	0-0	---		3-3	1-0	0-1	2-3
	1-1	1-1	1-1	2-1	0-3	0-1	2-0		2-2	3-0	1-2	0-1
Kilmarnock FC	0-0	1-4	---	1-0	2-1	1-0	3-1	---		3-1	2-0	1-3
	4-2	0-1	2-1	3-2	1-1	2-4	2-2	2-2		3-0	4-1	2-3
Livingston FC	---	0-2	3-1	0-1	0-1	2-3	---	2-1	---		0-1	---
	0-0	0-5	1-0	1-1	0-2	1-4	1-2	1-1	0-3		1-2	2-2
Motherwell FC	---	1-3	2-0	2-3	3-1	---	2-2	0-1	---	2-1		---
	3-1	4-4	4-5	1-0	5-0	1-1	1-3	0-2	2-2	1-0		0-1
Rangers FC	1-1	0-1	---	1-0	---	2-0	2-0	---	4-0	4-1	1-0	
	0-0	3-1	3-0	5-1	2-2	1-0	0-3	1-1	3-0	3-0	2-0	

Scottish Premier League

Season 2005/2006

Celtic	38	28	7	3	93	37	91
Hearts	38	22	8	8	71	31	74
Rangers	38	21	10	7	67	37	73
Hibernian	38	17	5	16	61	56	56
Kilmarnock	38	15	10	13	63	64	55
Aberdeen	38	13	15	10	46	40	54
Inverness Caledonian Thistle	38	15	13	10	51	38	58
Motherwell	38	13	10	15	55	61	49
Dundee United	38	7	12	19	41	66	33
Falkirk	38	8	9	21	35	64	33
Dunfermline	38	8	9	21	33	68	33
Livingston	38	4	6	28	25	79	18

With 5 games of the season left, the Division was split into two groups of 6. The top half contended for the Championship while the bottom half decided relegation.

Scottish Football League Division One Season 2005/2006	Airdrie United	Brechin City	Clyde	Dundee	Hamilton Academical	Queen of the South	Ross County	St. Johnstone	St. Mirren	Stranraer
Airdrie United FC	■	3-3	1-1	7-0	0-0	1-1	2-3	2-1	1-4	3-0
	■	6-0	1-3	4-0	2-2	4-0	0-1	3-1	0-1	1-0
Brechin City FC	0-0	■	3-1	0-3	0-1	1-1	3-3	0-2	0-3	0-0
	1-1	■	1-1	1-3	1-2	1-1	1-4	1-4	2-3	2-3
Clyde FC	3-1	5-1	■	3-3	2-2	3-0	2-0	2-3	0-1	1-1
	1-0	2-1	■	1-1	1-1	1-0	1-0	0-1	1-2	1-0
Dundee FC	2-3	0-1	0-1	■	2-4	2-3	0-0	0-1	4-0	2-1
	0-2	1-0	3-3	■	1-1	3-1	0-0	2-1	3-2	1-1
Hamilton Academical FC	1-0	2-0	2-0	0-0	■	0-2	0-0	1-2	0-0	1-0
	1-1	3-0	1-1	1-1	■	5-2	2-1	0-1	3-1	2-0
Queen of the South FC	2-0	0-0	2-1	1-3	1-1	■	0-0	3-2	0-0	1-0
	1-0	0-0	1-2	0-0	1-2	■	2-3	1-3	0-1	1-1
Ross County FC	0-1	2-0	0-1	0-0	2-1	3-1	■	2-2	0-2	1-1
	2-2	1-0	3-1	3-0	0-0	1-1	■	2-1	0-4	2-1
St. Johnstone FC	2-2	3-0	1-0	0-0	1-1	2-1	1-1	■	0-0	3-2
	1-0	3-1	0-0	1-1	5-1	4-0	1-1	■	1-2	1-1
St. Mirren FC	2-1	3-2	2-1	2-1	0-2	1-0	0-1	0-1	■	3-1
	1-1	1-0	2-0	0-0	2-1	2-0	2-0	0-0	■	0-0
Stranraer FC	1-1	2-0	0-5	1-1	5-4	1-0	2-2	0-2	0-1	■
	1-0	1-1	1-2	0-0	1-2	0-0	2-3	1-1	1-2	■

Scottish League Division One

Season 2005/2006

St. Mirren	36	23	7	6	52	28	76
St. Johnstone	36	18	12	6	59	34	66
Hamilton Academical	36	15	14	7	53	39	59
Ross County	36	14	14	8	47	40	56
Clyde	36	15	10	11	54	42	55
Airdrie United	36	11	12	13	57	43	45
Dundee	36	9	16	11	43	50	43
Queen of the South	36	7	12	17	31	54	33
Stranraer	36	5	14	17	33	53	29
Brechin City	36	2	11	23	28	74	17

Scottish Football League Division Two Season 2005/2006	Alloa Athletic	Ayr United	Dumbarton	Forfar Athletic	Gretna	Greenock Morton	Partick Thistle	Peterhead	Raith Rovers	Stirling Albion
Alloa Athletic FC		1-1	1-0	0-1	0-3	0-0	2-1	0-2	1-1	0-0
		0-4	1-4	1-1	0-3	0-3	1-6	4-1	1-2	2-4
Ayr United FC	0-1		2-0	0-1	2-4	1-1	1-2	1-2	0-0	3-0
	1-1		2-0	2-1	1-3	0-1	2-2	1-1	2-1	2-5
Dumbarton FC	0-1	4-5		0-0	0-2	0-2	2-3	2-3	0-1	3-2
	1-1	6-0		2-0	0-1	1-1	1-2	1-0	1-2	2-0
Forfar Athletic FC	3-0	1-0	2-3		2-1	0-2	0-0	0-1	0-2	1-2
	3-1	1-2	2-0		1-3	0-1	2-3	3-2	5-2	3-0
Gretna FC	2-1	3-0	3-0	1-2		1-2	6-1	3-1	2-1	6-0
	4-0	2-2	1-0	5-1		3-1	2-2	3-0	5-1	1-0
Greenock Morton FC	4-1	0-4	4-0	3-0	2-2		1-0	0-0	2-0	1-0
	5-2	2-1	4-0	1-0	0-2		2-1	2-1	2-0	1-2
Partick Thistle FC	2-3	2-2	2-1	1-0	0-2	1-1		0-1	1-0	0-3
	4-3	1-0	3-2	1-0	3-3	2-0		1-3	1-3	0-0
Peterhead FC	3-0	1-2	3-1	1-1	1-3	2-1	2-1		0-0	2-0
	3-1	3-3	1-0	4-2	0-2	1-0	1-1		0-1	1-3
Raith Rovers FC	0-1	1-1	0-0	1-0	0-1	1-1	1-2	1-0		2-3
	4-2	3-3	3-2	0-2	1-3	1-2	1-1	0-2		5-2
Stirling Albion FC	0-0	1-0	3-1	3-1	2-1	3-1	1-2	2-1	2-2	
	1-2	3-3	0-0	4-2	0-5	0-2	1-2	1-3	1-0	

Scottish League Division Two

Season 2005/2006

Gretna	36	28	4	4	97	30	88
Greenock Morton	36	21	7	8	58	33	70
Peterhead	36	17	6	13	53	47	57
Partick Thistle	36	16	9	11	57	56	57
Stirling Albion	36	15	6	15	54	63	51
Ayr United	36	10	12	14	56	61	42
Raith Rovers	36	11	9	16	44	54	42
Forfar Athletic	36	12	4	20	44	55	40
Alloa Athletic	36	8	8	20	36	77	32
Dumbarton	36	7	5	24	40	63	26

Scottish Football League Division Three Season 2005/2006	Albion Rovers	Arbroath	Berwick Rangers	Cowdenbeath	East Fife	East Stirling.	Elgin City	Montrose	Queen's Park	Stenhousemuir
Albion Rovers FC		0-2	0-1	1-3	3-1	2-0	1-2	1-1	1-0	1-2
		2-2	0-2	0-3	2-4	4-2	0-2	1-1	1-1	0-2
Arbroath FC	1-0		0-2	4-1	2-1	2-1	0-1	3-0	1-0	3-2
	1-2		4-0	0-3	1-0	7-2	2-0	2-1	1-1	1-1
Berwick Rangers FC	2-1	2-1		1-0	1-1	1-0	1-1	1-1	1-0	3-0
	0-1	3-0		1-0	3-0	3-2	3-1	1-1	1-2	0-2
Cowdenbeath FC	2-1	4-2	1-1		4-1	5-0	2-1	2-0	6-0	1-1
	2-1	3-2	0-1		3-1	5-1	5-2	2-0	0-2	4-1
East Fife FC	1-0	0-3	1-0	2-1		1-2	0-2	4-0	0-1	2-1
	1-1	1-1	0-4	1-0		3-1	1-2	3-2	1-0	2-3
East Stirlingshire FC	1-0	0-4	0-1	1-1	2-1		0-2	1-0	0-0	0-7
	3-1	3-1	1-2	0-1	1-2		0-2	1-1	0-4	0-0
Elgin City FC	2-1	4-1	1-3	0-4	5-3	3-0		1-0	1-2	0-2
	2-2	2-0	2-2	0-3	1-2	1-1		0-0	2-2	1-2
Montrose FC	2-2	0-1	1-2	0-3	0-2	2-0	1-3		0-0	0-2
	0-2	1-0	0-0	0-1	3-1	3-0	2-0		0-1	0-3
Queen's Park FC	1-1	0-0	0-1	2-2	1-1	3-1	3-3	2-2		2-0
	3-1	2-2	1-3	0-2	2-0	3-0	3-0	0-3		1-2
Stenhousemuir FC	4-2	0-0	1-0	1-2	4-2	5-0	1-2	5-1	1-2	
	1-0	2-0	0-1	2-0	2-1	6-1	3-1	6-2	1-0	

Scottish League Division Three

Season 2005/2006

Cowdenbeath	36	24	4	8	81	34	76
Berwick Rangers	36	23	7	6	54	27	76
Stenhousemuir	36	23	4	9	78	38	73
Arbroath	36	16	7	13	57	47	55
Elgin City	36	15	7	14	55	58	52
Queen's Park	36	13	12	11	47	42	51
East Fife	36	13	4	19	48	64	43
Albion Rovers	36	7	8	21	39	60	29
Montrose	36	6	10	20	31	59	28
East Stirlingshire	36	6	5	25	28	89	23

Scottish Premier League 2006/2007 Season	Aberdeen	Celtic	Dundee United	Dunfermline Athletic	Falkirk	Heart of Midlothian	Hibernian	Inverness C.T.	Kilmarnock	Motherwell	Rangers	St. Mirren
Aberdeen	■	0-1	3-1	1-0	2-1	1-3	2-1	1-1	3-1	2-1	1-2	2-0
	■	1-2	2-4	3-0		1-0	2-2	1-1	3-0		2-0	
Celtic	1-0	■	2-2	1-0	1-0	2-1	2-1	3-0	4-1	2-1	2-0	2-0
	2-1	■		2-1		1-3	1-0		2-0	1-0	0-1	5-1
Dundee United	3-1	1-4	■	0-0	1-2	0-1	0-3	3-1	1-0	1-1	2-1	1-0
		1-1	■	0-0	1-5		0-0	1-1		1-1		0-2
			■						0-0			
Dunfermline Athletic	0-3	1-2	2-1	■	0-3	1-2	0-4	0-0	3-2	0-2	1-1	2-1
			1-0	■	0-3	0-1	1-0		1-1	4-1	0-1	0-0
Falkirk	0-2	0-1	5-1	1-0	■	1-1	2-1	3-1	1-2	0-1	1-0	1-1
	1-2	1-0	2-0	1-0	■		1-0		0-2	1-2		2-0
					■							0-2
Heart of Midlothian	0-1	2-1	4-0	1-1	0-0	■	3-2	4-1	0-2	4-1	0-1	0-1
	1-1	1-2	0-4		1-0	■	2-0	1-0	1-0			1-1
Hibernian	1-1	2-2	2-1	2-0	0-1	2-2	■	2-0	2-2	3-1	2-1	5-1
	0-0	2-1		2-0	0-1		■	0-1	2-0	0-2		
							■				3-3	
Inverness Caledonian Thistle	1-1	1-1	0-0	1-0	3-2	0-0	0-0	■	3-4	0-1	2-1	1-2
		1-2	1-0	1-3	1-1		3-0	■		2-0		2-1
				2-1				■				
Kilmarnock	1-0	1-2	0-0	5-1	2-1	0-0	2-1	1-1	■	1-2	2-2	1-1
	1-2	1-2	1-0			1-0	0-2	3-2	■		1-3	
Motherwell	0-2	1-1	2-3	2-1	4-2	0-1	1-6	1-4	5-0	■	1-2	0-0
	0-2			2-0	3-3	0-2		1-0	0-1	■	0-1	2-3
Rangers	1-0	1-1	2-2	2-0	4-0	2-0	3-0	0-1	3-0	1-1	■	1-1
	3-0	2-0	5-0		2-1	0-0		1-1	0-1		■	
						2-1					■	
St. Mirren	1-1	1-3	1-3	0-0	1-0	2-2	1-0	1-1	0-1	2-0	2-3	■
	0-2		0-1	0-1			1-1	0-1	0-2	0-0	0-1	■

Scottish Premier League

Season 2006/2007

Celtic	38	26	6	6	65	34	84
Rangers	38	21	9	8	61	32	72
Aberdeen	38	19	8	11	55	38	65
Heart of Midlothian	38	17	10	11	47	35	61
Kilmarnock	38	16	7	15	47	54	55
Hibernian	38	13	10	15	56	46	49
Falkirk	38	15	5	18	49	47	50
Inverness Caledonian Thistle	38	11	13	14	42	48	46
Dundee United	38	10	12	16	40	59	42
Motherwell	38	10	8	20	41	61	38
St. Mirren	38	8	12	18	31	51	36
Dunfermline Athletic	38	8	8	22	26	55	32

With 5 games of the season left, the Division was split into two groups of 6. The top half contended for the Championship while the bottom half decided relegation.

78

Scottish Football League Division One 2006/2007 Season	Airdrie United	Clyde	Dundee	Gretna	Hamilton Academical	Livingston	Partick Thistle	Queen of the South	Ross County	St. Johnstone
Airdrie United		2-1	0-1	4-2	1-2	0-1	1-2	2-2	0-2	2-1
		1-0	0-3	0-0	1-0	3-1	1-1	0-3	0-1	1-2
Clyde	0-0		2-1	1-2	2-1	1-1	0-0	4-0	3-0	1-0
	0-1		1-1	2-0	3-0	0-1	2-0	0-1	2-4	0-1
Dundee	1-0	3-0		1-3	1-1	0-1	0-1	2-1	3-1	1-1
	2-1	1-4		0-1	1-0	2-0	3-1	1-0	3-2	2-1
Gretna	0-2	3-3	0-4		6-0	1-1	4-0	5-0	2-1	2-0
	0-0	0-0	1-0		1-0	4-1	2-0	0-3	4-1	0-2
Hamilton Academical	2-1	3-1	1-0	3-1		1-1	1-2	1-1	0-0	2-2
	3-0	1-1	1-0	0-0		3-0	2-1	2-2	1-0	3-4
Livingston	3-0	1-1	2-3	1-2	0-1		2-2	2-0	0-0	1-1
	1-3	0-0	1-3	1-1	1-2		0-1	0-1	1-1	3-2
Partick Thistle	4-2	1-1	3-1	0-6	3-1	2-3		1-1	3-2	1-5
	0-1	0-4	2-1	2-2	0-2	0-0		0-0	1-1	2-0
Queen of the South	1-1	0-2	2-0	0-3	1-1	2-0	0-2		2-0	0-1
	0-3	0-0	2-2	0-4	1-1	1-1	4-3		2-0	1-0
Ross County	2-1	1-1	1-0	0-1	0-1	0-3	2-5	1-0		2-2
	1-1	2-2	0-0	2-3	4-1	0-2	2-1	1-0		1-1
St. Johnstone	1-0	0-0	2-1	3-3	0-0	1-2	2-0	5-0	3-1	
	4-3	2-1	2-0	2-1	4-2	1-2	2-0	3-0	2-1	

Scottish League Division One

Season 2006/2007

Gretna	36	19	9	8	70	40	66
St. Johnstone	36	19	8	9	65	42	65
Dundee	36	16	5	15	48	42	53
Hamilton Academical	36	14	11	11	46	47	53
Clyde	36	11	14	11	46	35	47
Livingston	36	11	12	13	41	46	45
Partick Thistle	36	12	9	15	47	63	45
Queen of the South	36	10	11	15	34	54	41
Airdrie United	36	11	7	18	39	50	40
Ross County	36	9	10	17	40	57	37

Scottish Football League Division Two 2006/2007 Season	Alloa Athletic	Ayr United	Brechin City	Cowdenbeath	Forfar Athletic	Greenock Morton	Peterhead	Raith Rovers	Stirling Albion	Stranraer
Alloa Athletic		0-1	2-2	2-1	2-0	3-2	1-1	1-2	1-2	1-1
		1-1	2-3	0-0	2-0	0-3	2-4	2-3	1-1	1-0
Ayr United	0-1		1-2	0-4	5-0	0-1	1-2	1-0	0-0	0-2
	4-3		1-1	0-2	3-1	1-0	0-0	0-2	3-2	1-0
Brechin City	2-0	0-2		4-2	4-2	2-3	1-0	1-0	0-1	3-0
	2-3	2-0		1-0	2-2	0-1	3-1	1-2	1-4	1-1
Cowdenbeath	6-1	1-1	1-3		3-2	1-2	4-2	1-2	2-2	4-2
	5-2	3-1	0-3		2-1	1-1	0-3	1-5	1-2	0-0
Forfar Athletic	0-2	0-1	1-2	1-1		1-3	2-3	1-1	0-2	2-1
	0-2	1-1	3-2	2-0		0-4	1-2	1-2	0-2	5-0
Greenock Morton	4-0	0-0	1-0	1-0	1-1		4-2	2-0	1-1	3-0
	2-1	4-2	0-2	3-0	9-1		2-1	1-0	2-1	1-1
Peterhead	1-2	3-1	1-1	1-0	8-0	0-4		0-1	2-3	5-2
	0-0	2-2	1-4	0-2	2-2	1-2		0-0	2-1	5-0
Raith Rovers	0-0	1-0	1-1	1-3	0-0	1-3	5-2		1-3	1-1
	3-0	0-1	1-0	1-2	2-1	2-0	2-0		0-1	0-0
Stirling Albion	5-0	1-3	2-1	1-0	3-0	2-1	2-0	1-1		3-3
	4-0	4-2	0-1	1-0	4-0	2-1	2-1	0-1		0-2
Stranraer	2-2	1-3	3-1	1-0	3-2	0-3	2-1	1-4	2-1	
	3-4	0-3	0-2	1-6	4-1	2-1	1-1	0-2	3-1	

Scottish League Division Two

Season 2006/2007

Team	P	W	D	L	F	A	Pts
Greenock Morton	36	24	5	7	76	32	77
Stirling Albion	36	21	6	9	67	39	69
Raith Rovers	36	18	8	10	50	33	62
Brechin City	36	18	6	12	61	45	60
Ayr United	36	14	8	14	46	47	50
Cowdenbeath	36	13	6	17	59	56	45
Alloa Athletic	36	11	9	16	47	70	42
Peterhead	36	11	8	17	60	62	41
Stranraer	36	10	9	17	45	74	39
Forfar Athletic	36	4	7	25	37	90	19

Scottish Football League Division Three 2006/2007 Season	Albion Rovers	Arbroath	Berwick Rangers	Dumbarton	East Fife	East Stirlingshire	Elgin City	Montrose	Queen's Park	Stenhousemuir
Albion Rovers		1-3	0-1	2-1	0-1	4-0	3-1	3-1	1-1	2-5
		0-3	0-1	0-1	0-3	2-1	6-2	2-2	2-1	2-1
Arbroath	2-3		0-1	0-0	1-1	1-2	2-1	3-1	1-2	2-0
	0-0		1-0	2-2	1-3	3-2	2-1	1-0	1-0	4-1
Berwick Rangers	1-1	3-2		3-0	2-1	2-2	3-1	1-2	1-0	0-1
	3-0	1-0		2-1	2-0	2-0	0-0	1-0	0-2	2-1
Dumbarton	3-1	0-2	2-0		2-1	2-0	3-1	2-0	0-0	4-0
	3-1	1-0	1-2		0-2	2-1	1-0	2-1	1-2	1-1
East Fife	2-2	2-1	2-0	1-0		5-0	1-1	2-0	1-0	0-0
	1-3	1-2	0-2	1-0		0-2	3-1	2-0	1-0	1-1
East Stirlingshire	0-1	0-2	0-1	0-2	0-4		2-1	0-3	2-1	5-0
	0-0	1-5	0-3	1-5	0-2		0-2	0-2	0-2	0-1
Elgin City	0-3	0-4	1-2	0-2	1-2	5-0		3-2	1-2	2-0
	3-0	0-1	2-1	0-1	2-3	2-1		0-2	0-3	2-1
Montrose	2-1	0-1	0-1	1-1	1-0	1-0	2-0		0-3	0-1
	2-3	0-1	1-2	0-5	3-3	4-0	0-1		0-2	3-2
Queen's Park	2-1	0-3	1-0	1-0	3-0	1-3	3-0	1-1		1-1
	5-0	1-0	0-2	2-0	1-1	2-1	3-0	5-0		1-0
Stenhousemuir	3-2	1-2	2-3	1-0	0-1	2-0	2-0	5-0	2-1	
	0-4	1-2	2-0	5-1	3-5	1-1	3-2	2-5	1-2	

Scottish League Division Three

Season 2006/2007

Berwick Rangers	36	24	3	9	51	29	75
Arbroath	36	22	4	10	61	33	70
Queen's Park	36	21	5	10	57	28	68
East Fife	36	20	7	9	59	37	67
Dumbarton	36	18	5	13	52	37	59
Albion Rovers	36	14	6	16	56	61	48
Stenhousemuir	36	13	5	18	53	63	44
Montrose	36	11	4	21	42	62	37
Elgin City	36	9	2	25	39	69	29
East Stirlingshire	36	6	3	27	27	78	21

Highland Football League 2006/2007 Season	Brora Rangers	Buckie Thistle	Clachnacuddin	Cove Rangers	Deveronvale	Forres Mechanics	Fort William	Fraserburgh	Huntly	Inverurie Loco Works	Keith	Lossiemouth	Nairn County	Rothes	Wick Academy
Brora Rangers		1-4	1-1	2-1	0-5	2-6	3-2	2-0	2-7	0-2	1-3	2-1	2-4	3-0	0-1
Buckie Thistle	5-1		1-1	0-0	1-0	3-3	4-1	1-2	2-0	1-1	2-0	3-0	2-1	3-2	4-1
Clachnacuddin	5-0	0-1		2-2	2-3	2-1	0-3	3-0	1-1	2-3	0-1	3-1	2-1	0-3	1-2
Cove Rangers	5-0	0-2	1-2		2-2	3-3	6-3	2-1	5-1	1-0	0-2	2-1	2-1	1-0	5-0
Deveronvale	7-0	1-1	2-1	2-1		4-2	7-1	1-1	4-0	0-1	1-2	4-2	7-2	1-3	3-1
Forres Mechanics	3-1	2-2	0-1	2-3	3-3		1-2	0-0	3-1	0-1	1-1	4-1	1-4	3-1	2-2
Fort William	2-4	0-2	0-5	0-4	0-5	0-6		0-2	2-3	1-3	1-5	2-3	0-3	0-5	2-4
Fraserburgh	4-1	2-0	3-0	0-2	0-4	5-0	2-0		1-1	2-3	1-2	2-2	3-2	6-1	4-3
Huntly	3-0	2-2	1-1	2-0	1-0	3-1	3-0	5-0		1-0	2-1	4-0	3-0	3-4	4-3
Inverurie Loco Works	3-2	3-1	2-0	1-1	2-1	2-1	5-0	0-0	4-5		2-1	4-0	1-1	3-1	5-2
Keith	2-1	3-0	1-0	4-0	3-1	4-2	9-1	2-2	2-1	1-2		3-1	3-0	1-0	3-0
Lossiemouth	1-1	0-1	3-3	1-0	1-2	1-2	1-2	1-1	0-4	0-3	0-2		1-1	2-0	0-1
Nairn County	6-2	1-1	2-1	0-2	0-1	4-0	4-0	1-3	1-0	1-2	2-2	3-0		4-0	3-0
Rothes	0-2	0-2	3-2	1-1	2-3	1-0	3-1	2-0	0-4	5-1	2-2	2-0	0-2		0-1
Wick Academy	1-2	0-3	0-2	1-0	0-3	3-2	5-0	1-1	0-2	2-3	0-2	3-1	1-3	6-1	

Highland Football League

Season 2006/2007

Team	P	W	D	L	GF	GA	Pts
Keith	28	20	4	4	67	26	64
Inverurie Loco Works	28	20	4	4	62	33	64
Buckie Thistle	28	16	8	4	54	28	56
Deveronvale	28	17	4	7	77	35	55
Huntly	28	17	4	7	67	39	55
Cove Rangers	28	13	6	9	52	36	45
Nairn County	28	13	4	11	57	42	43
Fraserburgh	28	11	8	9	48	42	41
Clachnacuddin	28	9	6	13	43	42	33
Rothes	28	10	2	16	42	57	32
Wick Academy	28	10	2	16	44	61	32
Forres Mechanics	28	7	7	14	54	60	28
Brora Rangers	28	8	2	18	38	84	26
Lossiemouth	28	3	5	20	25	64	14
Fort William	28	3	0	25	26	107	9

Scottish League Challenge Cup 2006

Round	Date	Home	Score	Away	Score	
Round 1	16th Aug 2006	Airdrie United	0	Gretna	3	
Round 1	15th Aug 2006	Ayr United	2	Livingston	1	
Round 1	15th Aug 2006	Brechin City	1	Arbroath	2	
Round 1	15th Aug 2006	Cowdenbeath	4	Stirling Albion	0	
Round 1	15th Aug 2006	Dumbarton	1	Greenock Morton	2	(aet)
Round 1	15th Aug 2006	East Stirlingshire	0	Queen's Park	5	
Round 1	16th Aug 2006	East Fife	0	Ross County	3	
Round 1	16th Aug 2006	Elgin City	2	Stenhousemuir	0	
Round 1	15th Aug 2006	Forfar Athletic	2	Dundee	1	
Round 1	15th Aug 2006	Hamilton Academical	3	Berwick Rangers	1	
Round 1	16th Aug 2006	Montrose	2	Peterhead	0	
Round 1	15th Aug 2006	Partick Thistle	1	Albion Rovers	2	
Round 1	15th Aug 2006	Queen of the South	1	Stranraer	0	
Round 1	15th Aug 2006	St. Johnstone	3	Raith Rovers	1	(aet)
Round 2	29th Aug 2006	Albion Rovers	5	Elgin City	2	
Round 2	29th Aug 2006	Forfar Athletic	1	Arbroath	3	
Round 2	30th Aug 2006	Gretna	3	Hamilton Academical	1	
Round 2	30th Aug 2006	Montrose	0	Clyde	3	
Round 2	29th Aug 2006	Greenock Morton	3	Cowdenbeath	2	
Round 2	30th Aug 2006	Queen of the South	2	Ayr United	2	(aet)
		Ayr United won on penalties				
Round 2	29th Aug 2006	Ross County	2	Alloa Athletic	1	(aet)
Round 2	29th Aug 2006	St. Johnstone	3	Queen's Park	0	
Round 3	12th Sep 2006	Albion Rovers	3	Arbroath	3	(aet)
		Albion Rovers won on penalties				
Round 3	12th Sep 2006	Clyde	1	Ayr United	0	
Round 3	12th Sep 2006	Greenock Morton	3	St. Johnstone	2	
Round 3	12th Sep 2006	Ross County	3	Gretna	2	(aet)
Semi-Final	27th Sep 2006	Clyde	3	Greenock Morton	1	
Semi-Final	27th Sep 2006	Ross County	4	Albion Rovers	1	
FINAL	12th Nov 2006	Ross County	1	Clyde	1	(aet)
		Ross County won on penalties				

Scottish Cup 2006/2007

Round	Date	Home		Away		
Round 1	18th Nov 2006	Arbroath	2	Albion Rovers	1	
Round 1	18th Nov 2006	Brechin City	1	Queen's Park	1	
Round 1	18th Nov 2006	Deveronvale	3	Montrose	2	
Round 1	25th Nov 2006	East Stirlingshire	0	Stirling Albion	2	
Round 1	18th Nov 2006	East Fife	1	Berwick Rangers	3	
Round 1	18th Nov 2006	Edinburgh University	2	Keith	1	
Round 1	18th Nov 2006	Preston Athletic	2	Stenhousemuir	0	
Round 1	18th Nov 2006	Stranraer	4	Alloa Athletic	2	
Replay	28th Nov 2006	Queen's Park	1	Brechin City	2	
Round 2	9th Dec 2006	Annan Athletic	0	Greenock Morton	3	
Round 2	9th Dec 2006	Berwick Rangers	2	Arbroath	0	
Round 2	9th Dec 2006	Brechin City	2	Preston Athletic	1	
Round 2	9th Dec 2006	Cowdenbeath	5	Edinburgh University	1	
Round 2	9th Dec 2006	Deveronvale	2	Fraserburgh	1	
Round 2	9th Dec 2006	Edinburgh City	0	Stirling Albion	1	
Round 2	9th Dec 2006	Elgin City	1	Buckie Thistle	0	
Round 2	9th Dec 2006	Peterhead	0	Ayr United	2	
Round 2	9th Dec 2006	Raith Rovers	0	Dumbarton	1	
Round 2	9th Dec 2006	Stranraer	3	Forfar Athletic	1	
Round 3	10th Jan 2007	Aberdeen	2	Hibernian	2	
Round 3	6th Jan 2007	Airdrie United	0	Motherwell	1	
Round 3	6th Jan 2007	Berwick Rangers	0	Falkirk	2	
Round 3	6th Jan 2007	Celtic	4	Dumbarton	0	
Round 3	6th Jan 2007	Clyde	0	Gretna	3	
Round 3	6th Jan 2007	Cowdenbeath	1	Brechin City	1	
Round 3	6th Jan 2007	Deveronvale	5	Elgin City	4	
Round 3	6th Jan 2007	Dundee	1	Queen of the South	1	
Round 3	16th Jan 2007	Dundee United	3	St. Mirren	2	
Round 3	7th Jan 2007	Dunfermline Athletic	3	Rangers	2	
Round 3	6th Jan 2007	Hamilton Academical	2	Livingston	4	
Round 3	6th Jan 2007	Greenock Morton	3	Kilmarnock	1	
Round 3	6th Jan 2007	Ross County	0	Partick Thistle	1	
Round 3	6th Jan 2007	St. Johnstone	0	Ayr United	0	
Round 3	6th Jan 2007	Stirling Albion	1	Inverness Caledonian Thistle	6	
Round 3	6th Jan 2007	Stranraer	0	Heart of Midlothian	4	
Replay	17th Jan 2007	Ayr United	1	St. Johnstone	2	(aet)
Replay	16th Jan 2007	Brechin City	0	Cowdenbeath	1	
Replay	18th Jan 2007	Hibernian	4	Aberdeen	1	
Replay	16th Jan 2007	Queen of the South	3	Dundee	3	(aet)
		Queen of the South won on penalties				
Round 4	3rd Feb 2007	Deveronvale	0	Partick Thistle	1	
Round 4	3rd Feb 2007	Dunfermline Athletic	1	Heart of Midlothian	0	
Round 4	3rd Feb 2007	Falkirk	0	St. Johnstone	3	
Round 4	3rd Feb 2007	Hibernian	3	Gretna	1	
Round 4	3rd Feb 2007	Inverness Caledonian Thistle	1	Dundee United	0	
Round 4	4th Feb 2007	Livingston	1	Celtic	4	
Round 4	3rd Feb 2007	Motherwell	2	Greenock Morton	0	
Round 4	3rd Feb 2007	Queen of the South	2	Cowdenbeath	0	

Round 5	24th Feb 2007	Dunfermline Athletic	2	Partick Thistle	0
Round 5	25th Feb 2007	Inverness Caledonian Thistle	1	Celtic	2
Round 5	28th Feb 2007	Motherwell	1	St. Johnstone	2
Round 5	24th Feb 2007	Queen of the South	1	Hibernian	2
Semi-Final	14th Apr 2007	Celtic	2	St. Johnstone	1
Semi-Final	15th Apr 2007	Dunfermline Athletic	0	Hibernian	0
Replay	24th Apr 2007	Dunfermline Athletic	1	Hibernian	0
FINAL	26th May 2007	Celtic	1	Dunfermline Athletic	0

Cup Statistics provided by:

www.soccerdata.com

Scottish League Cup 2006/2007

Round 1	8th Aug 2006	Albion Rovers	1	Stenhousemuir	2	
Round 1	9th Aug 2006	Arbroath	0	Elgin City	1	
Round 1	9th Aug 2006	Ayr United	2	Berwick Rangers	0	
Round 1	8th Aug 2006	Brechin City	2	Greenock Morton	1	
Round 1	8th Aug 2006	Cowdenbeath	4	East Stirlingshire	1	
Round 1	8th Aug 2006	Dumbarton	3	Stirling Albion	0	
Round 1	8th Aug 2006	Dundee	1	Partick Thistle	3	
Round 1	8th Aug 2006	Forfar Athletic	1	Alloa Athletic	2	(aet)
Round 1	9th Aug 2006	Montrose	1	Peterhead	3	(aet)
Round 1	8th Aug 2006	Queen of the South	4	Clyde	2	
Round 1	8th Aug 2006	Queen's Park	2	Hamilton Academical	1	(aet)
Round 1	8th Aug 2006	Raith Rovers	1	Airdrie United	2	
Round 1	8th Aug 2006	Ross County	4	Stranraer	2	
Round 1	8th Aug 2006	St. Johnstone	3	East Fife	1	
Round 2	22nd Aug 2006	Alloa Athletic	2	Ross County	1	
Round 2	22nd Aug 2006	Ayr United	0	Dunfermline Athletic	0	(aet)
		Dunfermline Athletic won on penalties				
Round 2	22nd Aug 2006	Brechin City	0	Livingston	3	
Round 2	22nd Aug 2006	Cowdenbeath	0	Falkirk	5	
Round 2	22nd Aug 2006	Dundee United	1	Airdrie United	0	(aet)
Round 2	22nd Aug 2006	Hibernian	4	Peterhead	0	
Round 2	23rd Aug 2006	Inverness Caledonian Thistle	3	Dumbarton	1	
Round 2	22nd Aug 2006	Motherwell	3	Partick Thistle	2	
Round 2	22nd Aug 2006	Queen of the South	1	Kilmarnock	2	(aet)
Round 2	22nd Aug 2006	Queen's Park	0	Aberdeen	0	(aet)
		Queen's Park won on penalties				
Round 2	22nd Aug 2006	St. Mirren	3	Stenhousemuir	1	
Round 2	22nd Aug 2006	St. Johnstone	4	Elgin City	0	
Round 3	20th Sep 2006	Alloa Athletic	0	Heart of Midlothian	4	
Round 3	19th Sep 2006	Celtic	2	St. Mirren	0	
Round 3	20th Sep 2006	Dunfermline Athletic	0	Rangers	2	
Round 3	20th Sep 2006	Hibernian	6	Gretna	0	
Round 3	19th Sep 2006	Inverness Caledonian Thistle	0	Falkirk	1	
Round 3	19th Sep 2006	Kilmarnock	2	Livingston	1	(aet)
Round 3	20th Sep 2006	Queen's Park	0	Motherwell	3	
Round 3	19th Sep 2006	St. Johnstone	3	Dundee United	0	
Round 4	7th Nov 2006	Celtic	1	Falkirk	1	(aet)
		Falkirk won on penalties				
Round 4	8th Nov 2006	Hibernian	1	Heart of Midlothian	0	
Round 4	7th Nov 2006	Kilmarnock	3	Motherwell	2	
Round 4	8th Nov 2006	Rangers	0	St. Johnstone	2	
Semi-Final	30th Jan 2007	Kilmarnock	3	Falkirk	0	
Semi-Final	31st Jan 2007	St. Johnstone	1	Hibernian	3	(aet)
FINAL	18th Mar 2007	Hibernian	5	Kilmarnock	1	

SCOTLAND INTERNATIONAL LINE-UPS AND STATISTICS 2002

16th May 2002
v SOUTH KOREA *Busan*

Sullivan	Tottenham Hotspur
Dailly	West Ham United
Weir	Everton
Ross	Rangers
Caldwell	Newcastle United
G. Alexander	Preston N.E. (sub. Stockdale 62)
Gemmill	Everton
Stewart	Manchester Utd. (sub. Severin 46)
Johnston	Middlesbrough (sub. Kyle 65)
Dobie	West Bromwich Albion
O'Connor	Hibernian (sub. Williams 46)

Result 1-4   Dobie

20th May 2002
v SOUTH AFRICA *Hong Kong*

Douglas	Celtic
Stockdale	Middlesbrough (sub. Alexander 69)
Caldwell	Newcastle United (sub. Wilkie 46)
Dailly	West Ham United
Weir	Everton
Ross	Rangers
Gemmill	Everton (sub. Stewart 86)
Williams	Nottingham Forest (sub Severin 78)
Dobie	West Bromwich Albion
Kyle	Sunderland
Johnston	Middlesbrough (sub McFadden 62)

Result 0-2

21st August 2002
v DENMARK *Hampden Park*

Douglas	Celtic
Ross	Rangers
Weir	Everton (sub. Severin 78)
Dailly	West Ham United
Stockdale	Middlesbro' (sub. Alexander 72)
Ferguson	Rangers
Lambert	Celtic (sub. McInnes 81)
McNaughton	Aberdeen (sub. Crainey 46)
Naysmith	Everton (sub. Johnston 73)
Kyle Kevin	Sunderland
Thompson	Rangers (sub. Dobie 56)

Result 0-1

7th September 2002
v FAROE ISLANDS (ECQ) *Toftir*

Douglas	Celtic
Ross	Rangers (sub. Alexander 75)
Crainey	Celtic
Dailly	West Ham United
Weir	Everton
Ferguson	Rangers
Dickov	Leicester City (sub. Crawford 46)
Dobie	West Brom. (sub. Thompson 83)
Kyle	Sunderland
Lambert	Celtic
Johnston	Middlesbrough

Result 2-2   Lambert, Ferguson

12th October 2002
v ICELAND (ECQ) *Reykjavik*

Douglas	Celtic
Ross	Rangers
Wilkie	Dundee
Pressley	Heart of Midlothian
Dailly	West Ham United
Ferguson	Rangers
McNamara	Celtic (sub. Davidson 34)
Crawford	Dunfermline Athletic
Thompson	Rangers (sub. Severin 85)
Lambert	Celtic
Naysmith	Everton (sub. Anderson 89)

Result 2-0   Dailly 6, Naysmith 63

15th October 2002
v CANADA *Edinburgh*

P. Gallacher	Dundee United
Dailly	West Ham United
Pressley	Heart of Midlothian
Wilkie	Dundee (sub. Murray 75)
Anderson	Aberdeen
Alexander	Preston North End
Gemmill	Everton (sub. Severin 66)
Devlin	Birmingham City
Ross	Rangers (sub. Davidson 45)
Crawford	Dunfermline Athletic (sub. Kyle 89)
Thompson	Rangers (sub. McFadden 81)

Result 3-1   Crawford 2, Thompson

20th November 2002
v PORTUGAL   *Braga*

Douglas	Celtic
Anderson	Aberdeen (sub. McInnes 24)
Pressley	Heart of Midlothian
Wilkie	Dundee (sub. Severin 83)
Alexander	Preston North End
Lambert	Celtic (sub. Williams 78)
Dailly	West Ham United
Naysmith	Everton
Ross	Rangers (sub. Devlin 46)
Dobie	West Brom. Albion (sub. Kyle 78)
Crawford	Dunfermline Athletic

Result 0-2

12th February 2003
v EIRE   *Hampden Park*

Sullivan	Tottenham H. (sub. Gallacher 45)
Caldwell	Newcastle United
Anderson	Aberdeen
Dailly	West Ham United
Alexander	Preston North End
Lambert	Celtic (sub. Gemmill 45)
Ferguson	Rangers (sub. Cameron 65)
Naysmith	Everton
McCann	Rangers (sub. Smith 65)
Crawford	Dunfermline (sub. Thompson 65)
Hutchison	West Ham United (sub. Devlin 45)

Result 0-2

29th March 2003
v ICELAND (ECQ)   *Hampden Park*

Douglas	Celtic
Wilkie	Dundee
Pressley	Heart of Midlothian
Dailly	West Ham United
Alexander	Preston North End
Ferguson	Rangers
Lambert	Celtic
Hutchison	West Ham United (sub. Devlin 82)
Naysmith	Everton
Miller	Wolves (sub. McNamara 82)
Crawford	Dunfermline Athletic

Result 2-1   Miller, Wilkie

2nd April 2003
v LITHUANIA (ECQ)   *Kaunas*

P. Gallacher	Dundee United
Pressley	Heart of Midlothian
Dailly	West Ham United
Wilkie	Dundee
Alexander	Preston North End
Lambert	Celtic
McNamara	Celtic (sub. Gray 78)
Naysmith	Everton
Hutchison	West Ham Utd. (sub. Cameron 85)
Miller	Wolverhampton Wanderers
Crawford	Dunfermline Ath. (sub. Devlin 57)

Result 0-1

30th April 2003
v AUSTRIA   *Hampden Park*

P. Gallacher	Dundee United
Wilkie	Dundee
Webster	Heart of Midlothian
Pressley	Heart of Midlothian
Devlin	Birmingham City (sub. Smith 84)
Burley	Derby County (sub. Cameron 64)
Dailly	West Ham Utd. (sub. Gemmill 45)
Hutchison	West Ham United (sub. Miller 62)
Naysmith	Everton
Thompson	Rangers (sub. Crawford 45)
McFadden	Motherwell

Result 0-2

27th May 2003
v NEW ZEALAND   *Edinburgh*

Douglas	Celtic
Ross	Rangers (sub. Alexander 45)
Naysmith	Everton
Webster	Heart of Midlothian
Pressley	Heart of Midlothian
Dailly	West Ham United
Devlin	Birmingham City
McNamara	Celtic (sub. Kerr 82)
Kyle	Sunderland (sub. Gray 59)
Crawford	Dunfermline Athletic
McFadden	Motherwell

Result 1-1   Crawford

SCOTLAND INTERNATIONAL LINE-UPS AND STATISTICS 2003

7th June 2003
v GERMANY (ECQ) *Hampden Park*

Douglas	Celtic
Ross	Rangers (sub. McNamara 74)
Pressley	Heart of Midlothian
Webster	Heart of Midlothian
Naysmith	Everton
Devlin	Birmingham City (sub. Rae 60)
Lambert	Celtic
Cameron	Wolverhampton Wanderers
Dailly	West Ham United
Crawford	Dunfermline Athletic
Miller	Wolves (sub. Thompson 90)

Result 1-1   Miller

20th August 2003
v NORWAY   *Oslo*

Douglas	Celtic
Ross	Rangers (sub. Fletcher 60)
Naysmith	Everton
Pressley	Heart of Midlothian
Webster	Heart of Midlothian
Ferguson	Rangers
Lambert	Celtic
Dailly	West Ham United
Hutchison	West Ham United
Crawford	Dunfermline Ath. (sub. Devlin 79)
Cameron	Wolverhampton W. (sub. Rae 84)

Result 0-0

6th September 2003
v FAROE ISLANDS (ECQ) *Hampden*

Douglas	Celtic
McNamara	Celtic
Naysmith	Everton
Webster	Heart of Midlothian
Wilkie	Dundee
Ferguson	Rangers
Devlin	Birmingham City (sub. McFadden 59)
Cameron	Wolverhampton Wanderers
Dickov	Leicester City (sub. Rae 68)
Crawford	Dunfermline Ath. (sub. Thompson 75)
McCann	Southampton

Result 3-1   McCann, Dickov, McFadden

10th September 2003
v GERMANY (WCQ)   *Dortmund*

Douglas	Celtic
McNamara	Celtic
Naysmith	Everton
Dailly	West Ham United
Pressley	Heart of Midlothian
Ferguson	Blackburn Rovers
McFadden	Everton (sub. Rae 52)
Cameron	Wolverhampton Wanderers
Thompson	Rangers
McCann	Southampton
Lambert	Celtic (sub. Ross 46)

Result 1-2   McCann

11th October 2003
v LITHUANIA (ECQ)   *Hampden Park*

Douglas	Celtic
McNamara	Celtic
Naysmith	Everton
Dailly	West Ham United
Pressley	Heart of Midlothian
Ferguson	Blackburn Rovers
Rae	Dundee
Cameron	Wolves (sub. Fletcher 65)
Miller	Wolves (sub. Hutchison 65)
Crawford	Dunfermline Athletic
McFadden	Everton (sub. Alexander 89)

Result 1-0   Fletcher

15th November 2003
v NETHERLANDS (EC Play-off)
Hampden Park

Douglas	Celtic
McNamara	Celtic
Naysmith	Everton
Pressley	Heart of Midlothian
Wilkie	Dundee
Ferguson	Blackburn Rovers
Fletcher	Manchester United
Dailly	West Ham United
Dickov	Leicester City (sub. Miller 65)
McFadden	Everton (sub. Hutchison 89)
McCann	Southampton (sub. Pearson 70)

Result 1-0   McFadden

SCOTLAND INTERNATIONAL LINE-UPS AND STATISTICS 2003-2004

19th November 2003
v NETHERLANDS (EC Play-off) *Amsterdam*

Douglas	Celtic
McNamara	Celtic
Naysmith	Everton (sub. Ross 46)
Pressley	Heart of Midlothian
Wilkie	Dundee
Ferguson	Blackburn Rovers
Fletcher	Manchester United
Rae	Dundee
Dickov	Leicester City (sub. Crawford 46)
McFadden	Everton
McCann	Southampton (sub. Miller 62)

Result 0-6
Netherlands won 6-1 on aggregate

18th February 2004
v WALES *Millennium Stadium, Cardiff*

Douglas	Celtic
McNamara	Celtic
Naysmith	Everton (sub. Murty 46)
Dailly	West Ham United
Caldwell	Newcastle United
Ritchie	Walsall
Fletcher	Manchester Utd. (sub Webster 85)
Cameron	Wolves (sub. Gallagher 67)
Miller	Wolverhampton Wanderers
Dickov	Leicester City
Pearson	Celtic (sub. McFadden 46)

Result 0-4

31st March 2004
v ROMANIA *Hampden Park*

Gallacher	Dundee United
Alexander	Preston North End
Kennedy	Celtic (sub. Crainey 17)
Dailly	West Ham United
Pressley	Heart of Midlothian
G. Caldwell	Hibernian
Rae	Rangers
Cameron	Wolverhampton Wanderers
Thompson	Rangers (sub. Crawford 63)
Miller	Wolves (sub. McFadden 50)
McCann	Southampton

Result 1-2   McFadden

28th April 2004
v DENMARK   *Copenhagen*

Gallacher	Dundee United
G. Caldwell	Hibernian
Crainey	Southampton
Dailly	West Ham United
Mackay	Norwich City
Pressley	Heart of Midlothian
Fletcher	Manchester United
Holt	Norwich City (sub. Canero 16)
Kyle	Sunderland
McFadden	Everton
Cameron	Wolves (sub. McCann 46)

Result 0-1

27th May 2004
v ESTONIA   *Tallinn*

Gallacher	Dundee United
McNamee	Livingston
Hughes	Portsmouth
G. Caldwell	Hibernian
Mackay	Norwich City
Pressley	Hearts (sub. Webster 46)
Fletcher	Manchester United
Holt	Norwich City
Miller	Wolves (sub. Crawford 79)
McFadden	Everton (sub. Kerr 89)
Quashie	Portsmouth

Result 1-0   McFadden

30th May 2004
v TRINIDAD & TOBAGO
Easter Road, Edinburgh

Gordon	Heart of Midlothian
McNamara	Celtic
McAllister	Livingston
G. Caldwell	Hibernian (sub. S. Caldwell 78)
Mackay	Norwich City (sub. McNamee 85)
Pressley	Heart of Midlothian
Fletcher	Manchester United
Holt	Norwich City (sub. Kerr 54)
Crawford	Dunfermline Ath. (sub. Miller 67)
McFadden	Everton (sub. Webster 85)
Quashie	Portsmouth (sub. Hughes 71)

Result 4-1   Fletcher, Holt, Caldwell, Quashie

SCOTLAND INTERNATIONAL LINE-UPS AND STATISTICS 2004

18th August 2004
v HUNGARY   *Hampden Park*

Marshall	Celtic
Holt	Norwich City
Naysmith	Everton
Webster	Heart of Midlothian
Pressley	Heart of Midlothian
Ferguson	Blackburn Rov. (sub. Severin 71)
Fletcher	Man. United (sub. Pearson 73)
G. Caldwell	Hibernian (sub. Thompson 46)
Miller	Wolves (sub. Crawford 57)
McFadden	Everton
Quashie	Portsmouth

Result 0-3

3rd September 2004
v SPAIN   *Valencia*

Gordon	Heart of Midlothian
G. Caldwell	Hibernian
Naysmith	Everton
Webster	Heart of Midlothian
Mackay	Norwich City
Ferguson	Blackburn Rovers
Fletcher	Man. United (sub. Cameron 57)
McNamara	Celtic
Crawford	Plymouth Argyle (sub. Miller 57)
Quashie	Portsmouth
McFadden	Everton (sub. Pearson 46)

Result 1-1   (The match was abandoned after 59 minutes due to floodlight failure)

8th September 2004
v SLOVENIA (WCQ)   *Hampden Park*

Gordon	Heart of Midlothian
G. Caldwell	Hibernian
Naysmith	Everton (sub. Holt 58)
Webster	Heart of Midlothian
Mackay	Norwich City
Ferguson	Blackburn Rovers
Fletcher	Manchester United
McNamara	Celtic
Dickov	Blackburn Rov. (sub. Crawford 79)
Quashie	Portsmouth
McFadden	Everton

Result 0-0

9th October 2004
v NORWAY (WCQ)   *Hampden Park*

Gordon	Heart of Midlothian
G. Caldwell	Hibernian
Naysmith	Everton
Anderson	Aberdeen
Webster	Heart of Midlothian
Ferguson	Blackburn Rovers
Fletcher	Manchester United
Holt	Norwich City (sub. Thompson 80)
Dickov	Blackburn Rovers (sub. Miller 74)
McFadden	Everton
Hughes	Portsmouth (sub. Pearson 62)

Result 0-1

13th October 2004
v MOLDOVA (WCQ)   *Chisinau*

Gordon	Heart of Midlothian
G. Caldwell	Hibernian
Naysmith	Everton (sub. Murray 46)
S. Caldwell	Sunderland
Webster	Heart of Midlothian
Ferguson	Blackburn Rovers
Fletcher	Manchester United (sub. Miller 65)
Holt	Norwich City
Thompson	Rangers (sub. McCulloch 85)
Crawford	Plymouth Argyle
Cameron	Wolverhampton Wanderers

Result 1-1   Thompson

17th November 2004
v SWEDEN   *Easter Road, Edinburgh*

Marshall	Celtic
McNaughton	Aberdeen
Murray	Hibernian
Anderson	Aberdeen
Webster	Hearts (sub. Hammell 54)
McNamara	Celtic (sub. Severin 64)
Nicholson	Dunfermline Athletic
Quashie	Portsmouth (sub. Hughes 89)
Miller	Wolves (sub. Crawford 71)
McFadden	Everton
Pearson	Celtic

Result 1-4   McFadden (pen)

SCOTLAND INTERNATIONAL LINE-UPS AND STATISTICS 2005

26th March 2005
v ITALY (WCQ)   *Milan*

Douglas	Celtic (sub. Gordon 39)
McNamara	Celtic
Pressley	Heart of Midlothian
Weir	Heart of Midlothian
Naysmith	Everton
Hartley	Hearts (sub. McCann 76)
Ferguson	Rangers
G. Caldwell	Hibernian
Quashie	Southampton
McCulloch	Wigan Athletic
Miller	Wolves (sub. O'Connor 86)

Result 0-2

4th June 2005
v MOLDOVA (WCQ) *Hampden Park*

Gordon	Heart of Midlothian
Alexander	Preston North End
McNamara	Celtic (sub. Dailly 25)
Pressley	Heart of Midlothian
D. Weir	Everton
Ferguson	Rangers
Fletcher	Manchester United
Webster	Heart of Midlothian
Miller	Wolverhampton Wanderers
Hartley	Heart of Midlothian
McCulloch	Wigan Ath. (sub. McFadden 73)

Result 2-0   Dailly, McFadden

8th June 2005
v BELARUS (WCQ)   *Minsk*

Gordon	Heart of Midlothian
D. Weir	Everton
Pressley	Heart of Midlothian
Webster	Heart of Midlothian
G. Caldwell	Hibernian
Dailly	West Ham United
Fletcher	Manchester United
Ferguson	Rangers
Alexander	Preston North End
McCulloch	Wigan Ath. (sub. McFadden 76)
K. Miller	Wolverhampton Wanderers

Result 0-0

17th August 2005
v AUSTRIA   *Graz*

Gordon	Hearts (sub. Douglas 46)
McNamara	Wolverhampton Wanderers
Alexander	Preston North End
Pressley	Hearts (sub. Anderson 46)
S. Caldwell	Sunderland
Webster	Heart of Midlothian
K. Miller	Wolves (sub. Riordan 46)
Dailly	West Ham United
O'Connor	Hibernian
O'Neil	Preston N.E. (sub. Severin 46)
Quashie	Southampton (sub. Hughes 73)

Result 2-2   Miller, O'Connor

3rd September 2005
v ITALY (WCQ)   *Hampden Park*

Gordon	Heart of Midlothian
McNamara	Wolverhampton Wanderers
Webster	Heart of Midlothian
Dailly	West Ham United
Weir	Everton
Ferguson	Rangers
Fletcher	Manchester United
Alexander	Preston North End
K. Miller	Wolves (sub. Beattie 75)
Hartley	Heart of Midlothian
Quashie	(Southampton (sub. McCann 66)

Result 1-1   Miller

7th September 2005
v NORWAY (WCQ)   *Oslo*

Gordon	Heart of Midlothian
McNamara	Wolverhampton Wanderers
Webster	Heart of Midlothian
Pressley	Heart of Midlothian
Weir	Everton
Ferguson	Rangers
Fletcher	Manchester United
Alexander	Preston North End
K. Miller	Wolves (sub. McCann 40)
Hartley	Heart of Midlothian
McFadden	Everton (sub. Beattie 71)

Result 2-1   Miller 2

8th October 2005
v BELARUS (WCQ) *Hampden Park*

Gordon	Heart of Midlothian
Alexander	Preston North End
Murray	Rangers (sub. Maloney 46)
Pressley	Heart of Midlothian
Weir	Everton
Ferguson	Rangers
Fletcher	Manchester United
Dailly	West Ham United
K. Miller	Wolverhampton Wanderers
Hartley	Heart of Midlothian
McCulloch	Wigan Athletic

Result 0-1

12th October 2005
v SLOVENIA (WCQ) *Celje*

Gordon	Heart of Midlothian
Dailly	West Ham United
Alexander	Preston North End
Pressley	Hearts (sub. G. Caldwell 46)
Weir	Everton
Webster	Heart of Midlothian
Fletcher	Manchester United
Quashie	Southampton (sub. S. Caldwell 71)
K. Miller	Wolves (sub. O'Connor 46)
Hartley	Heart of Midlothian
McFadden	Everton

Result 3-0   Fletcher, McFadden, Hartley

12th November 2005
v U.S.A. *Hampden Park*

Gordon	Heart of Midlothian
Dailly	West Ham United
Alexander	Preston North End
Pressley	Hearts (sub. S. Caldwell 46)
Webster	Heart of Midlothian
Weir	Everton (sub. G. Caldwell 46)
Fletcher	Manchester United
Hartley	Heart of Midlothian
O'Connor	Hibernian (sub. Maloney 73)
Quashie	Southampton (sub. Brown 73)
McCann	Southampton (sub. McFadden 62)

Result 1-1   Webster

1st March 2006
v SWITZERLAND *Hampden Park*

Gordon	Hearts (sub. N. Alexander 46)
Dailly	West Ham United
G. Alexander	Preston North End
Weir	Everton (sub. S. Caldwell 46)
Webster	Heart of Midlothian
Ferguson	Rangers (sub. Teale 46)
Fletcher	Manchester United
G. Caldwell	Hibernian
Miller	Wolverhampton Wanderers
Quashie	West Bromwich Albion
McFadden	Everton

Result 1-3   Miller

11th May 2006
v BULGARIA *Kobe, Japan*

N. Alexander	Cardiff City
Weir	Everton
Naysmith	Everton
Fletcher	Manchester United
G. Caldwell	Hibernian
Severin	Aberdeen (sub. Rae 69)
Anderson	Aberdeen
McCulloch	Wigan Athletic (sub. Murray 78)
Murty	Reading (sub. McNamee 82)
Teale	Wigan Athletic (sub. Burke 74)
Boyd	Rangers (sub. McFadden 52)

Result 5-1   Boyd 2, McFadden, Burke 2

13th May 2006
v JAPAN *Saitama, Japan*

N. Alexander	Cardiff City
Weir	Everton
Naysmith	Everton (sub. Murray 46)
McFadden	Everton (sub. Boyd 59)
Fletcher	Manchester United
G. Caldwell	Hibernian
Severin	Aberdeen (sub. Rae 46)
Anderson	Aberdeen
McCulloch	Wigan Athletic (sub. Miller 69)
Murty	Reading (sub. McNamee 79)
Teale	Wigan Athletic (sub. Burke 59)

Result 0-0

2nd September 2006
v FAROE ISLANDS (ECQ)   *Celtic Park*

Gordon	Heart of Midlothian
Dailly	West Ham United
Weir	Everton
Pressley	Heart of Midlothian
Naysmith	Everton
Fletcher	Manchester United (sub. Teale 46)
Hartley	Heart of Midlothian
Quashie	West Brom. Albion (sub Severin 84)
Miller	Celtic (sub. O'Connor 62)
Boyd	Rangers
McFadden	Everton

Result 6-0   Fletcher, McFadden, Boyd 2 (1 pen), Miller (pen), O'Connor

6th September 2006
v LITHUANIA (ECQ)   *Kaunas*

Gordon	Heart of Midlothian
Dailly	West Ham United
Naysmith	Everton
Pressley	Heart of Midlothian
Weir	Everton
G. Caldwell	Celtic
Fletcher	Manchester United
Hartley	Heart of Midlothian (sub. Severin 88)
Miller	Celtic
Quashie	West Brom. Albion (sub. Boyd 42)
McFadden	Everton (sub G. Alexander 22)

Result 2-1   Dailly, Miller

7th October 2006
v FRANCE (ECQ)   *Hampden Park*

Gordon	Heart of Midlothian
Dailly	West Ham United
Alexander	Preston North End
Pressley	Heart of Midlothian
Weir	Everton
Ferguson	Rangers
Fletcher	Manchester United
G. Caldwell	Celtic
McFadden	Everton (sub. O'Connor 71)
Hartley	Heart of Midlothian
McCulloch	Wigan Athletic (sub. Teale 57)

Result 1-0   Caldwell

11th October 2006
v UKRAINE (ECQ)   *Kiev*

Gordon	Heart of Midlothian
Neilson	Hearts (sub. McManus 89)
Alexander	Preston North End
Pressley	Heart of Midlothian
Weir	Everton
Ferguson	Rangers
Fletcher	Manchester United
G. Caldwell	Celtic
Miller	Celtic
Hartley	Heart of Midlothian
McFadden	Everton (sub. Boyd 73)

Result 0-2

24th March 2007
v GEORGIA (ECQ)   *Hampden Park*

Gordon	Heart of Midlothian
Alexander	Preston North End
Naysmith	Everton
Weir	Rangers
McManus	Celtic
Ferguson	Rangers
Teale	Derby County (sub. Brown 59)
Hartley	Celtic
Miller	Celtic (sub. Maloney 90)
Boyd	Rangers (sub. Beattie 76)
McCulloch	Wigan Athletic

Result 2-1   Boyd, Beattie

28th March 2007
v ITALY (ECQ)   *Bari*

Gordon	Heart of Midlothian
Alexander	Preston North End
Naysmith	Everton
Weir	Rangers
McManus	Celtic
Ferguson	Rangers
Teale	Derby County (sub. Maloney 65)
Hartley	Celtic
Miller	Celtic
Brown	Hibernian (sub. Beattie 85)
McCulloch	Wigan Athletic (sub. Boyd 80)

Result 0-2

30th May 2007
v AUSTRIA   *Vienna*

McGregor	Rangers (sub. Gordon 46)
Alexander	Preston North End (sub. Hutton 70)
Naysmith	Everton
G. Caldwell	Celtic
Weir	Rangers (sub. Dailly 46)
Ferguson	Rangers
Fletcher	Manchester United
Maloney	Aston Villa (sub. Adam 66)
Boyd	Rangers
O'Connor	Lokomotiv Moscow (sub. McManus 86)
McCulloch	Wigan Athletic (sub. Hartley 46)

Result 1-0   O'Connor

6th June 2007
v FAROE ISLANDS (ECQ)   *Toftir*

Gordon	Heart of Midlothian
Alexander	Preston North End
Naysmith	Everton
McManus	Celtic
Weir	Rangers
Ferguson	Rangers
Fletcher	Manchester United (sub. Teale 68)
Hartley	Celtic
Boyd	Rangers (sub. Naismith 82)
O'Connor	Lokomotiv Moscow
Maloney	Aston Villa (sub. Adam 77)

Result 2-0   Maloney, O'Connor

Supporters' Guides Series

This top-selling series has been published annually since 1982 and the new editions contain 2006/2007 Season's results and tables, Directions, Photos, Phone numbers, Parking information, Admission details, Disabled info and much more.

THE SUPPORTERS' GUIDE TO PREMIER & FOOTBALL LEAGUE CLUBS 2008

The 24th edition featuring all Premiership and Football League clubs.   *Price £6.99*

THE SUPPORTERS' GUIDE TO SCOTTISH FOOTBALL 2008

The 16th edition featuring all Scottish Premier League, Scottish League and Highland League clubs.   *Price £6.99*

THE SUPPORTERS' GUIDE TO NON-LEAGUE FOOTBALL 2008

This 16th edition covers all 68 clubs in Step 1 & Step 2 of Non-League football – the Football Conference National, Conference North and Conference South.   *Price £6.99*

THE SUPPORTERS' GUIDE TO NON-LEAGUE FOOTBALL 2007 – STEP 3 CLUBS

Following the reorganisation of Non-League Football the 3rd edition of this book features the 66 clubs which feed into the Football Conference.   *Price £6.99*

THE SUPPORTERS' GUIDE TO WELSH FOOTBALL GROUNDS 2007

The 11th edition featuring all League of Wales, Cymru Alliance & Welsh Football League Clubs + results, tables & much more.   *Price £6.99*

THE SUPPORTERS' GUIDE TO NORTHERN IRISH FOOTBALL 2007

This 4th edition features all Irish Premier League and Irish Football League Clubs + results, tables & much more.   *Price £6.99*

THE SUPPORTERS' GUIDE TO EIRCOM FAI CLUBS 2006

Back after a long absence this 4th edition features all Eircom League Premier and First Division Clubs + 10 years of results, tables & much more.   *Price £6.99*

These books are available UK & Surface post free from –

Soccer Books Limited (Dept. SBL)
72 St. Peter's Avenue
Cleethorpes
N.E. Lincolnshire